ERNEST HEMINGWAY

ERNEST HEMINGWAY
THE SEARCH FOR COURAGE

KEITH FERRELL

M. EVANS AND COMPANY, INC.
NEW YORK

Selections from the following works have been reprinted with the permission of Charles Scribner's Sons:

Ernest Hemingway, excerpt from *Across the River and Into the Trees.* Copyright 1950 Ernest Hemingway; copyright renewed 1978 Mary Hemingway.

Ernest Hemingway, excerpt from *By-line: Ernest Hemingway.* Copyright © 1967 Mary Hemingway.

Ernest Hemingway, excerpt from *Death in the Afternoon.* Copyright 1932 Charles Scribner's Sons; copyright renewed 1960 Ernest Hemingway.

Ernest Hemingway, resignation letter and excerpt from *Ernest Hemingway: Selected Letters 1917 to 1961*, edited by Carlos Baker. Copyright © 1981 The Ernest Hemingway Foundation, Inc.; copyright © 1981 Carlos Baker.

Ernest Hemingway, excerpt from *A Farewell to Arms.* Copyright 1929 Charles Scribner's Sons; copyright renewed 1957 Ernest Hemingway.

Ernest Hemingway, excerpt from *For Whom the Bell Tolls.* Copyright 1940 Ernest Hemingway; copyright renewed 1968 Mary Hemingway.

Ernest Hemingway, excerpt from *A Moveable Feast.* Copyright © 1964 Mary Hemingway.

Ernest Hemingway, excerpt from *The Old Man and the Sea.* Copyright 1952 Ernest Hemingway; copyright renewed 1980 Mary Hemingway.

Ernest Hemingway, excerpts from "Big Two-hearted River," "A Clean, Well-lighted Place," "Indian Camp," and "Up in Michigan" in *The Short Stories of Ernest Hemingway.* Copyright 1938 Ernest Hemingway; copyright renewed 1966 Mary Hemingway.

Ernest Hemingway, excerpt from *The Sun Also Rises.* Copyright 1926 Charles Scribner's Sons; copyright renewed 1954 Ernest Hemingway.

Ernest Hemingway, excerpt from *To Have and Have Not.* Copyright 1937 Ernest Hemingway; copyright renewed 1965 Mary Hemingway.

Carlos Baker, excerpt from "Wolves and Doughnuts" in *Ernest Hemingway: A Life Story.* Copyright © 1969 Carlos Baker; copyright © 1969 Mary Hemingway.

Library of Congress Cataloging in Publication Data
Ferrell, Keith.
  Ernest Hemingway: the search for courage.

  Bibliography: p.
  Includes index.
  Summary: A biography of the American author, detailing
his childhood, his marriages, the writing of his novels,
and his constant seeking to prove his courage.
  1. Hemingway, Ernest, 1899–1961—Biography—Juvenile
literature. 2. Novelists, American—20th century—
Biography—Juvenile literature. [1. Hemingway, Ernest,
1899–1961. 2. Authors, American] I. Title.
PS3515.E37Z5923 1984   813'.52 [B] [92] 84-10162

ISBN 0-87131-431-2

Copyright © 1984 by Keith Ferrell

M. Evans and Company, Inc.
216 East 49 Street
New York, New York 10017
Design by Diane Gedymin

Manufactured in the United States of America

9 8 7 6 5 4 3 2 1

FOR HARRY W. SPARROW, M.D.

CONTENTS

ONE

" 'FRAID A NOTHING!"

LIKE HIS FATHER, ERNEST HEMINGWAY always felt more at home in wilderness than in cities. The outdoors beckoned to him and even as a child he could not ignore its call. The trees and skies were filled with birds whose names he learned at an early age. The countryside bristled with wildlife that he learned to stalk and kill and dress out as meat for the table. A swiftly flowing stream was irresistible: there might be trout in it. And if not, it was still a stream, outside, *away*.

Ernest's father, Dr. Clarence Edmonds Hemingway, was a physician, a good one. He was also a dedicated outdoorsman who brought to the campsite the same discipline, sense of order, and methodical attention to detail that surgery demanded. His fishing and hunting companions looked to Ed Hemingway for instruction and example in the correct approach to setting up camp, finding good fishing spots, and living off the land. Ed Hemingway never failed and often delighted them.

He was a natural leader, a man of imposing presence, proud of his skills but modest about them. He would not show off or boast, preferring to use his abilities quietly and for the benefit of others. On one college camping trip, with food running short, he prepared a fresh blackberry pie from wild ingredients, using only rudimentary utensils. He located his own berries. He filled his hat with damp leaves, set them smoldering, and used the improvised smokepot to stun a hive of bees long enough to steal their honey. Though he had no use for alcoholic beverages, he

9

put an empty beer bottle to good purpose as a rolling pin, with a stripped log serving as his mixing board. The pie was baked beside the campfire, using an old piece of sheet metal to reflect heat. When the perfect pie was presented, Dr. Hemingway shrugged off his friends' praise. Every step had been accomplished efficiently and correctly. Anyone who would take the time could do what he had done. There was a right way and a wrong way of going about any endeavor, and Ed Hemingway made a point of always knowing the right way.

He was a man who did many things well, and he began acquiring his array of skills while young. Born in 1871, he was both athletic and studious as a boy. He enjoyed playing ball, but he was also a dedicated and careful observer of nature. He collected and catalogued Indian artifacts, and spent much of his free time roaming the burial mounds along the Des Plaines River outside Chicago. His hometown, Oak Park, was the most genteel of Chicago suburbs, but even so, when Ed Hemingway was young there was still a sense of the frontier about the town. Oak Park was surrounded by rolling hills, and wild chickens often wandered through the streets. Chicago was near, but so was wilderness. It was a wonderful place to grow up.

Occasionally there were problems. Ed Hemingway's parents instilled very strict codes of behavior in their children, and would tolerate no deviation from those codes. Once a group of bullies chased Ed into his own kitchen and proceeded to beat him badly while his mother stood watching, reminding her son of the virtue of turning the other cheek. The horror of that beating stayed with Ed Hemingway forever, and he had a lifelong hatred of physical violence.

The Hemingway family was wealthy, but Ed's parents respected the value of education, and along with their religious beliefs and moral convictions they passed on to their children a love of learning. Ed earned good grades in school, attended Oberlin College, and graduated at twenty-three from the medical college of the University of Chicago. He spent his internship in Scotland, at the University of Edinburgh. The Hemingways' fortunes had improved over the years, and when their son returned to Oak Park he opened his practice in their new home at 444 North Oak Park Avenue.

Although he came to earn a generous income, Dr. Hemingway gave little thought to monetary reward. When he designed a medical instrument—laminectomy forceps, which were an important contribution to the technology of spinal surgery—Dr. Hemingway refused to patent it. He felt it wrong to profit from an invention intended to benefit humanity.

His physical presence was as impressive as his moral stance. He was six feet tall, muscular and tanned from hours spent working in the sun. Upon discovering that some of his older patients were nervous about being treated by a doctor so youthful in appearance, he cultivated a neat black beard. Dr. Hemingway remained physically strong for much of his life, doing hours of hard manual labor for the simple enjoyment of it. Nothing, he believed, was better for the human body than honest sweat.

Such a talented and handsome young man naturally became the object of much attention from Oak Park's young women. He was quite a catch. Ed Hemingway, though, held firmly to the beliefs he'd learned as a child. He considered card playing, dancing, and parties sinful activities for decent people. He did not date, and refused to attend the social events to which other young men and women flocked. Even so attractive a high school classmate as Grace Hall, who lived at 439 North Oak Park Avenue, directly across the street from the doctor, could not tempt him to relax his convictions.

In 1894, not long after opening his practice, Dr. Hemingway undertook the care of Grace's mother, who was dying of cancer. His expert attention and gentle understanding became a great comfort to Grace.

Grace was a striking woman, as imposing in her own way as Ed. She was twenty-two when her mother's illness was diagnosed, and in the 1890s that was an age at which most women of good background were married or giving thought to marriage and the establishment of their own homes and families. Grace Hall was different: her poise and attitude toward life made her unlike any of her friends. She had no interest in domestic chores or goals. Grace had career plans of her own. She possessed a magnificent operatic voice, and dreamed of singing professionally. More than dreamed—she planned a career and was confident that she would become a star. And not just locally; Grace was eager for international success.

Grace's physique served to differentiate her from other women as well. She was tall, five feet eight inches, and she had an ample but attractive figure. She was not dwarfed by Dr. Hemingway, as were so many Oak Park girls.

Her adult size and robust constitution were a striking contrast to her childhood. When she was seven, Grace contracted scarlet fever and was blinded by it. Music was already the center of her life and she forced herself to learn to play the piano sightlessly. No handicap would get the better of Grace Hall. She never forgot the afternoon when, as she played, she realized that she could dimly see the piano keys. Over the next few weeks her vision returned, but her eyes had been permanently weakened.

It did not matter. Grace's discipline and willpower were strong. She knew she could accomplish whatever she set out to do. At a time when young ladies were meant to sit quietly with gloved hands folded, Grace donned a pair of her brother's knickers and rode his bicycle around the block. The family was scandalized, and Grace always claimed with some pride that she was the first female to ride a bicycle in Chicago.

Although bicycle riding may have been more than Grace's mother would tolerate, Mrs. Hall encouraged her daughter's ambitions. She kept Grace away from traditional girlish pursuits. Grace never learned to cook, never washed dishes or did laundry. Mrs. Hall maintained that such drudgery was unworthy of a person with Grace's gifts. Grace, said her mother, must give herself to music. And Grace did, growing more sure of herself each month. Even the cholera that struck her during high school did not make Grace morose. For six months she lay in bed planning her future and strengthening her determination. She not only regained her health, but during convalescence also gained six inches in height.

Now, in 1894, this tall and single-minded young woman found herself increasingly attracted to her mother's doctor. Grace and Dr. Hemingway spent a good deal of time together, first shyly renewing their acquaintanceship, soon falling in love. Early in 1895 they became engaged.

Mrs. Hall died in September of that year. Shortly afterward Grace left for New York to study opera under Madame Louisa Cappiani, a renowned vocal instructor. Madame Cappiani saw tremendous potential in Grace Hall, and lavished upon her all the attention and praise she possessed. Grace, Madame Cappiani proclaimed, would be known as the leading contralto of her generation. Her conviction was so strong that she would not accept tuition. Only when Grace earned enough from a single recital would Madame accept payment of her not inconsiderable bill.

That fee arrived with Grace's very first professional appearance. Grace earned more than one thousand dollars for a single concert given in Madison Square Garden in 1896. Her career, all agreed, was stunningly launched. But Grace's eyes, never fully recovered from the scarlet fever, could not tolerate the intense glare of stage lighting. Onstage, Grace was in constant pain, too much pain to be endured.

Her disappointment was bitter. Grace returned to Oak Park to prepare for her marriage. In the summer of 1896 her father took her to Europe for a tour of the Continent, a final trip together before her wedding. They visited many of the capitals, and Mr. Hall indulged his daughter's appreciation of life's finer things. He smiled as she displayed her sophistication. He let her spend freely for her trousseau. Before she was done Grace had assembled a large wardrobe, including nearly three dozen pairs of European gloves and almost as many hats.

Despite her disappointment, Grace did not neglect singing. She and her father toured concert halls, attended recitals, and met opera singers and conductors. Grace was even invited to perform for Queen Victoria, but a conflict in schedules prevented the royal concert. In late summer Grace and her father returned to Oak Park for the wedding.

The ceremony took place on October 1, 1896. Grace was the center of attention, her gown billowing with ninety yards of organdy. It had been decided that following their honeymoon the newlyweds would share the Halls' home with Grace's father. Ernest Hall had grown very fond of Dr. Hemingway, and took pains to welcome the young man into the family.

A room off the front stairs was organized as the doctor's office. Dr. Hemingway worked hard to establish his practice, and Grace quickly learned—and to a certain extent accepted—the inconveniences to which a physician's wife was subjected. Her husband was often called out in the middle of the night. Critically ill or dying patients depended upon the doctor for constant attention. For patients who had fallen upon hard times, Dr. Hemingway often performed surgery at no charge. He volunteered his skills at the local orphanage, delighting his young patients by bringing candy as well as medicine.

Dr. Hemingway earned a reputation for being a fine doctor and also a caring and humanitarian one. Because his practice was so new, his income rarely rose above fifty dollars a month. Grace, though, put her own talents to work, offering music lessons. It was not long before her income exceeded one thousand dollars a month. They had a comfortable life.

On January 15, 1898, their first child, a daughter, was born. It was a harrowing delivery. Dr. Hemingway was administering Grace's anesthesia when the attending obstetrician suffered a heart attack and collapsed. There was no one else in the house. Ed Hemingway never had greater call for concentration and discipline than that night as he delivered his own child, cared for his wife, and treated the obstetrician simultaneously. His belief in himself and his abilities was well-founded, and all three patients came through the ordeal.

The baby girl was named Marcelline. With her arrival the routine of the house began to change. While Grace enjoyed nursing her baby and dressing her in frilly gowns, she would have nothing to do with the more unpleasant aspects of motherhood, such as dirty diapers and soiled bedclothes. Those were left either to domestic help or to Dr. Hemingway, who handled them with his customary efficiency. Over the years he took on more and more of the responsibilities of the household. He did not seem to mind.

Early in 1899 Grace discovered that she was pregnant again. Both she and her husband hoped the second child would be a boy, and on July 21 their hopes were realized. Their son was delivered easily and without calamity. They named him Ernest Miller Hemingway, a strong name suitable for an infant who weighed nearly ten pounds and had thick black hair. Grace wrote in her diary, "the robins sang their sweetest songs to welcome the little stranger into this beautiful world."

The little stranger was not given a great deal of time to grow accustomed to the Oak Park corner of his new world. Before he was seven weeks old his parents took him and his older sister to northern Michigan, where Dr. Hemingway had purchased an acre of shorefront property on Walloon Lake.

It was quite a journey. From Chicago the family was carried by steamer virtually the entire length of Lake Michigan to the small town of Harbor Springs. From there the Hemingways traveled by rail to Petoskey, and then by a smaller branch line to Walloon Lake, which they crossed in a rowboat to reach their property.

Quite a journey, but worth it. Surrounded by hills thick with cedar, birches, and maples, Walloon Lake was a tranquil and isolated spot perfect for summer vacations. Petoskey, nine miles away, was the nearest community of any consequence, but a farmer lived less than a mile from the Hemingways' lot, close enough to be a convenient source of fresh milk and eggs.

The area was rich farm country, but it was even richer timberland. The whine of a sawmill could be heard almost every day. The mill was operated by Ottawa Indians, and the trees they worked were felled by Indians. Although the owners and managers of the logging business lived in nice cabins on the far side of Walloon Lake, the Indians lived in a camp of shacks not far from the Hemingways.

Dr. Hemingway's acre led down to a sandy beach ideal for children. The land was well shaded by large, spreading trees. Grace wanted the trees cut down: she felt trees were nothing more than breeding grounds for the insects she detested. Her husband refused to have the trees touched. They were part of the land and would remain so.

The Hemingways' first visit to Walloon Lake was brief. Grace held Ernest while the doctor made arrangements for the construction of the cabin that would be their summer home. A site was already prepared and the lumber, milled by the Indians, was neatly stacked nearby. The cabin would be ready for occupancy by the following summer. Baby Ernest barely had time for a glimpse of the lake before the family began the return journey to Oak Park.

On Grace's third wedding anniversary, October 1, 1899, her son was christened in the Congregational church. All through the fall Ernest grew. He ate on demand, whenever he wanted, and Grace felt that she could see his body getting stronger daily. In January 1900, before he was seven months old, Ernest cut his first tooth. Everyone agreed that this sturdy, bright-eyed baby was exceptional, with an exceptional future ahead.

Grace continued to give music lessons, but she also spent a good deal of time with her children. She thought of Ernest and Marcelline as twins, clothing them in identical dresses, brightening their long curls with identical ribbons. Occasionally she would dress them as boys, but more often they wore frocks. Their duplicate appearance delighted Grace and she loved to show them off. As was her nature, however, Grace would turn the children over to their father as soon as they were fussy or dirty.

The summer of 1900 was the Hemingways' first full season at Walloon Lake. The cabin was finished, a twenty-by-forty-foot structure with a large central fireplace flanked by window seats that doubled as beds. There were two bedrooms and a kitchen. Grace named the cottage Windemere, a romantic name that made her think of England, of stately homes and genteel society.

The land around Windemere was beautiful. Walloon Lake was fed by springs, its water cool and clear. There were plenty of fish in the lake, and the only real hazards were the half-submerged logs that had broken away from booms being towed to the mill. Sometimes one of these "deadheads" would drift onto the Hemingways' beach and Dr. Hemingway would saw it up for firewood.

Ernest and Marcelline flourished at Walloon Lake. The clean, fresh air was good for them, and they spent hours outside. Often they played naked on the beach, splashing and laughing, squealing with delight when their father treated them to rides in the washtub that doubled as the children's boat.

On July 13, a week before his first birthday, Ernest took his first steps. He was in a hurry to walk, to be free to wander through the hills, to explore the wonderful countryside. He cried when it was time for the family to return to Oak Park.

But there were delights to be found in Oak Park, too. Ernest loved to sit in his father's lap and look at the color plates in a book called *Birds of Nature*. They would turn the pages again and again and Dr. Hemingway would read Ernest the names of the birds. By the time he was one and a half, Ernest knew and could recognize seventy-three species of birds, calling out their Latin names when his father pointed to a picture.

It was not long before he spoke his first complete sentence: "I don't know Buffalo Bill!" Being so active, he probably made the statement with some regret. That first sentence unleashed a torrent of words. Ernest always had something to say. He quickly learned to recite heroic poetry, standing tall as he shouted out "The Charge of the Light Brigade" or "Hiawatha."

Although Grace continued to put ribbons in his hair and dresses on his stocky body, Ernest hated such pretense. He was a boy and he made that fact known. He preferred to dress as a cowboy and play with manly toys such as toy guns. He could often be seen stalking around the house as though hunting some large animal.

There were real animals at Walloon Lake, and each summer at Windemere brought Ernest into closer contact with the natural world. This was the world Ernest loved best. Grace might call the cottage Windemere; for Ernest, it was simply *wonderful*. The land was his and he walked over it boldly, hampered only by his parents' surveillance. At two he was ready to be out on his own.

During the final months of 1901, Grace again began to show signs of pregnancy. Ernest and Marcelline were impatient for the new arrival. Ernest badly wanted a younger brother, but on April 29, 1902, another girl was born. She was named Ursula. Ernest took one look at the baby and voiced the hope that his brother might arrive tomorrow.

Ernest, however, was boy enough for any family. A daredevil, he jumped and ran all over the place, although he was awkward and fell often. Nothing could deter him, nothing could slow him down. At Walloon Lake that summer he began putting his manliness to the test. He climbed trees and swung from limbs. He listened at night for the noises of animals. With an improvised musket he marched back and forth in front of Windemere, ready to defend the cottage against attackers. On his third birthday he caught his first fish. That summer he announced loudly the aspect of his personality of which he was most proud, the trait he felt was most important. "'Fraid a nothing!" he shouted, and shouted it again: "'Fraid a nothing!"

The following summer, 1903, Ernest came into his own in northern Michigan. He was four years old, old enough at last to be allowed some of the freedom he so desperately wanted. The culmination of the summer was his birthday, when his father took Ernest on an all-day fishing expedition.

The washtub boat had been replaced by a real vessel, a squat rowboat christened *Marcelline of Windemere.* Ernest and his sisters passed many pleasant hours in the boat, and even more dog-paddling in the shallow water near the shore. They giggled when Dr. Hemingway rowed Grace out to a point where she could lower herself over the side of the boat without her feet touching bottom. Although the lake floor was smooth and firm— one of the reasons Dr. Hemingway had been attracted to the land—Grace could not stand the thought of walking on it. It was bad enough to have to swim in water where fish lived.

Ernest loved to swim. And the trees that Grace loathed were among her son's most cherished spots. He learned to sit still, freezing himself until he nearly blended into the land. Sitting thus he could see squirrels and chipmunks and other small creatures—they would come almost up to him, nearly accepting him as one of their own.

Dr. Hemingway saw to it that Ernest's love of nature was not neglected in Oak Park. The doctor organized the Oak Park chapter of the Agassiz Club, a nature-study group. The club was named for Jean Louis Rodolphe Agassiz, a French naturalist who,after establishing the movement of glaciers and verifying the existence of ice ages in the earth's past, had come to America and devoted his life to the study of American wildlife and geology. Ernest and other children from the neighborhood followed Dr. Hemingway on carefully planned walks during which the doctor taught them how to observe, in a systematic way, the workings and wonders of the natural world. Ernest was learning lessons he would never forget.

TWO

LESSONS

NATURAL LESSONS WERE NOT the only ones Ernest was taught. As the children grew older, they were instructed and drilled in their responsibilities as a doctor's children. Especially important was their use of the telephone—they had to answer it the right way and immediately and accurately record all messages. When the children were using the phone they were under strict orders not to talk too long; someone with medical needs might be attempting to call in.

Interest in medicine and science was encouraged in Ernest not only through the Agassiz Club walks, but also through carefully chosen gifts. For his fifth birthday the boy was presented with a fine microscope, which his father taught him how to use. There was already talk in the family of Ernest's becoming a doctor.

The microscope was not Ernest's only tool for finding out about the world. His eyes and ears were sharp and he was not afraid to ask questions. Nor was he hesitant about arguing with anyone whose answers he did not trust. He was Ernest Hemingway and he wanted to know the truth. On one outing to the circus he encountered a three-legged man who was part of the show. Ernest listened to the man's statements and then, disbelieving what he had seen and heard, reached out and gave the questionable third leg a hard pinch. The man exclaimed in anger and Dr. Hemingway hustled Ernest off.

Ernest also studied music. Grace was not about to see her

children grow up without passing on to them as much of her love of music as she could. Both Ernest and Marcelline started piano lessons before they started school. Ernest resisted the lessons as much as possible, but Grace was adamant. He may not have enjoyed it, but he spent hours at the piano, and when he got older he was given cello lessons.

Mostly Ernest was full of spirit and energy. He took to concocting tall stories of the animals he encountered on his safaris through Oak Park's streets. Upon hearing one of these stories—a tale of Ernest single-handedly stopping a horse that was running wild—Grandfather Hall was prompted to comment on the boy's imagination. If Ernest put his gifts to good use, Grace's father said, he would grow up to be successful and famous. But if he did not, he would surely be put in jail.

While Ernest was receiving instruction in a variety of areas, his mother was once more adjusting to pregnancy. Again, family hopes for another boy rose. But on November 28, 1904, another Hemingway girl was born. She was named Madelaine, but because of her cheerful disposition she came to be known almost exclusively as "Sunny."

Not long after Sunny's birth it was discovered that Grandfather Hall was ill with Bright's disease, a very serious kidney disease. He never regained his health, and in the spring of 1905 he died. With her father's passing, Grace decided that she and her family had spent enough time in the Hall house. She put it on the market and purchased a large lot not far away. It was time, Grace announced, for the family to build their own home, one designed to her specifications.

The house was planned for ease of maintenance, with a kitchen whose efficiency was ahead of its time. The three-story house would have eight bedrooms. There would, of course, be a doctor's office and a reception room, but equally important to Grace was the music room she envisioned. It was to be a grand salon, the envy of every musician in Oak Park. Grace subscribed to a theory that stated that for perfect acoustics a music room should be half as tall as it was wide. Since the conservatory was to be a thirty-foot square, Grace insisted upon fifteen-foot ceilings. And when the house was finished, the music room lived up to Grace's expectations: she had never been in a home where music sounded so wonderful.

The new house would also have servants' quarters for the Hemingways' live-in staff of two. Grace remained determined to avoid domestic labor, and refused to consider homemaking without full-time servants. The servants accompanied the Hemingways to Walloon Lake each summer, their duties uninterrupted on vacation. When the new house was being designed and built, Windemere too was expanded for the growing Hemingway family and staff.

In October 1905, the Hemingways moved into a rented house that they would occupy until their new home was completed the following year. It was sad to move out of the house on North Oak Park Avenue. Ernest had many pleasant memories of his years there. The rented home did not have room for storage of all the Hemingway belongings, and Ernest would never forget standing beside his father as the doctor burned many of the zoological specimens he'd collected over the years. The alcohol in which the specimens were preserved made a lovely flame, and the specimens themselves sizzled and crackled as they burned.

It was in the fall of 1905 as well that Ernest entered first grade. Grace still dressed Ernest and Marcelline as twins. So determined was she to have the children thought of as twins that she held Marcelline out of school until Ernest was old enough to enter first grade beside her. Dr. Hemingway did not object to the pretense, although when the semester opened he did insist on having Ernest's long hair cut. Ernest's days of wearing dresses came to an end as well. He was six years old and it was time he looked like a boy.

Ernest adjusted easily to school. There was really no time for difficulty—the rented house was too small for the Hemingway family, and it seemed that they were constantly trying to stay out of one another's way. As the winter deepened the new house began to take shape, and by spring 1906 its shell was completed. In April a ceremony was held during which the structure was blessed by a minister. Grace sang a hymn to commemorate the occasion, and there were cakes and cookies for the children. The house would be ready for occupancy by the end of summer, after the family's return from Walloon Lake.

Dr. Hemingway's practice had grown enormously, and now it was impractical for him to spend the entire summer in northern Michigan. With the construction of the new house the family's overhead had grown considerably, and he had to spend a good portion of each summer in Oak Park to meet his financial obligations. Despite Grace's fear of wildlife and insects, she found that—with domestic help—she could manage the family quite well while her husband was away.

As the children grew older, the approach of summer was accompanied by almost unbearable excitement. They could not wait for the day they set out for Walloon Lake—it was their magic place. Over the years, arrival at the lake had settled into a brisk routine, with each member of the family assigned jobs and chores. While Dr. Hemingway climbed to the roof of the cottage to uncover the chimney, the children set to work raking the yard. Branches and limbs that had fallen during the winter had to be gathered and stacked neatly for firewood; leaves and debris had to be raked into piles for burning.

Within a few days of their arrival at the lake, a horsedrawn wagon would pull up, laden with crates of provisions that Dr. Hemingway had ordered before leaving Oak Park. The children's eyes grew wide as they watched their father check the boxes and cans against his inventory list—hams, cookies, jellies, chocolate. It was a treasure wagon, and the children understood that if they were good, and performed their tasks efficiently and without complaint, they would each receive a sweet surprise.

Dr. Hemingway enjoyed the delight his children took in

their rewards, but he knew the work he assigned them was a reward in itself. Only good could come to a person who acquired self-discipline, he believed. Discipline was even more important than knowledge. Exercise and hard work were keys to a long life; science had not developed, and would never develop, a better medicine than a day's labor.

Occasionally he felt obliged to reinforce his instruction with punishment. At such times Dr. Hemingway made his point with a stiff razor strap. When Grace spanked one of the children, she used the flat side of a hairbrush. Both parents followed spankings with prayer, kneeling with their children to ask God's forgiveness.

For all his high spirits, Ernest did not earn too many spankings. He was always harder on himself than his parents were, trying hard to perfect his abilities at any task he was assigned. He wanted to do well; he wanted his parents to be pleased. His mother noted in her diary with some pride that by the age of four Ernest had learned to recognize those times he'd done wrong, and would then find a switch and spank himself, sparing his mother the trouble.

None of the children misbehaved often. They understood their father's demands and expectations, and worked hard to live up to them. They also understood that Grace was in no way a traditional mother: they knew better than to bother her with childish complaints or requests.

The one thing Dr. Hemingway absolutely refused to tolerate was laziness, and he had a broad definition of it. He did not allow the children to sit still, and grew angry if he caught them relaxing or even reading. He knew that reading was important, but it was not so important as work, as hard physical activity. Ernest and his sisters loved to read, and quickly became adept at finding hiding places where they could lose themselves in a book without too much chance of being discovered.

Life at Walloon Lake was not all work, though, and Dr. Hemingway looked for ways of turning work into fun. Laundry day was a family activity, with the doctor supervising the washing of clothes and linens, and then gathering the children into their bathing suits to carry the soapy wash into the lake for rinsing. They would dip the clothes again and again into the clear water of the lake, splashing and giggling as they worked.

All of the children learned to swim, and their father drilled them repeatedly in lifesaving techniques. He rowed them out to deep water and then, without warning, tipped the rowboat over. The children had to stay afloat on their own, without life jackets or support. Dr. Hemingway remained close by, in the water himself, ready to help should a child get into serious difficulty, but not so close that the children might turn to him. Self-reliance, he taught, was the key to any situation.

Ernest did well in the capsizing lessons, and he was a good swimmer, but his first love was fishing. He could stand for hours, pole in hand, waiting for the tug of a fish. His favorite pastime of all was to accompany his father around the lake on a daylong fishing expedition, during which he listened attentively as the doctor spoke of the rules, codes, and manners of the sport. In fishing, as in all other worthwhile pursuits, there was a method, a body of correct knowledge that must be acquired and employed without exception. Ernest loved to fish, and he learned all the rules.

In the summer of 1905, Dr. Hemingway purchased Longfield Farm, a forty-acre tract across the lake from Windemere. The land was cultivated by a tenant who paid his rent with one-third of the harvest. The Hemingways planted scores of fruit trees there, and one of the children's most frequent chores was to make their way slowly through the orchard, weeding and watching for pests, which they dropped into cans of kerosene.

Longfield Farm was dominated by a high central hill that offered from its top a fine view of the countryside. The climb was steep but, the family agreed, the vista was a delight. Grace spoke frequently of building a new, more elaborate summer home on Red Top Mountain, as the hill was known. Her husband felt that one new house at a time was more than sufficient, and it was the house under construction in Oak Park that was on his mind.

That house was ready upon their return in the fall of 1906. The family settled into the big house quickly. Grace assumed her place of dominion in the large music room, and Dr. Hemingway treated patients in his office at the other end of the house. The children scurried between, laughing and playing.

Ernest was now in second grade. He proved himself an intelligent but not exceptional student. He took great pleasure in reading, but was less than first-rate in mathematics. Numbers could not hold his attention the way a narrative could. When there was no book at hand, his imagination served Ernest well. He could close his eyes and daydream of Walloon Lake, of the woods, of the wait for a fish's strike. Dr. Hemingway often reminded Ernest that daydreaming was no way to get ahead, that he should not waste his youth on idle fantasies. It was time for Ernest to begin building the foundation of his life; his imagination must be kept under control.

But the new house offered many temptations to a boy with an active imagination. The floor-to-ceiling mirror midway up the front staircase was a perfect place to practice boxing. Ernest passed many hours there, shirt off, throwing punches and feinting at his own reflection. Boxing was a new interest, and Ernest took it seriously. It, too, possessed a set of rules, a code by which participants must fight. Ernest learned the rules and attempted to abide by them.

There were other nice things about the house. It was large enough to afford more than one good spot for hiding with a book. After so much time in cramped quarters, Ernest especially enjoyed having his own bedroom. His room became a favorite meeting place for his friends: they shut the door and formed secret societies and organizations dedicated to mysterious pursuits. When they wanted a special thrill they crept down to the library, which doubled as the doctor's waiting room. Slowly they opened a closet door and peeked inside. There, eerily white in the darkness, hung an adult skeleton that Dr. Hemingway used for study and instruction. Around the house, when the door was shut, the skeleton was known as "Susie Bone-a-part." When the door was open, though, the skeleton was not so much of a joke, even for Ernest, who still loudly maintained that he was afraid of nothing.

As he grew older he sought more and more freedom to explore the world. He went for long walks through Oak Park. At that time, early in the century, Oak Park was considered the "middle-class capital of the world." Its streets were safe and clean, the majority of its houses spacious and comfortable, most of its residents prosperous and professional. Oak Park's residents were proud of their status, and the community's social order and hierarchy were well established. It was important to attend the right church, be a member of the most respectable institutions, and obey the social rules. In many ways Oak Park's order of society was similar to that which flourished in England during the reign of Queen Victoria. Manners and correct behavior were important; they made life pleasant. Perhaps most important of all was the sense of decorum and respectability that guided one's life. Rude language was never to be used. Vulgar ideas and attitudes were unheard of. Decency, cleanliness, and piety were the town's watchwords. Oak Park was a Victorian town with a Victorian society, and Dr. and Mrs. Clarence Hemingway were important members of that society.

But the world was changing, and as Ernest walked through Oak Park's streets he could see some of the changes. Horses and carriages were giving way to automobiles. Victorian architecture, ornate and rich with turnip turrets, carpenters' lace, porticoes, and balustrades, seemed quaint and old-fashioned compared to many of the buildings Ernest passed. Frank Lloyd Wright lived in Oak Park, and the great architect had designed more than one of the town's homes and buildings. Often long and low, clean and simple, with strong angles and huge picture

27

windows, Wright's designs created quite a contrast with traditional structures such as the new Hemingway home. Not far away from Ernest's home stood one of Wright's triumphs, Unity Temple. Ernest often strolled past the temple and stared at its lines.

Dr. and Mrs. Hemingway did not embrace the changes that were taking place. They had been shaped by their parents' values, and they impressed those values upon their children. Grace clung to Victorian fashion, wearing floor-length dresses and large feathered hats long after such clothing passed out of style.

Oak Park remained a pleasant place in which to grow up. It was a peaceful town but not a sleepy one, and Ernest found plenty to do. He often set out for all-day expeditions alone. Other times, his father would take the members of the Agassiz Club to the banks of the Des Plaines River for nature walks. Occasionally Ernest joined other children for a game of sandlot baseball, but not often. Despite his vigor and love of physical activity, Ernest was not well coordinated physically. His awkwardness was revealed on the field, and there was nothing Ernest hated more than looking foolish.

It also became evident that his eyesight was poor. His left eye dominated his right, and he had difficulty following a swiftly moving ball. He would not wear glasses. Grace, despite her own poor vision, felt that eyeglasses spoiled one's appearance. While her opposition was intended primarily for her daughters—a true lady would never hamper her beauty by wearing spectacles—Ernest shared her opinion. It was hard to look courageous with a pair of glasses perched on the bridge of his nose. His vanity, coupled with a deep admiration of his father's outstanding eyesight, prevented Ernest from ever being comfortable wearing glasses.

But baseball was not the only distraction a boy could find in Oak Park, and Ernest had no trouble filling his time. He was increasingly drawn to books, losing himself in stories of distant lands and interesting people. He continued to suffer through piano lessons, and Grace tried to enroll him in cello instruction. He practiced his boxing. There was school five days a week, and church on Sundays. Dr. Hemingway encouraged his son toward scientific pursuits, assisting him with his microscope, guiding him as they pored over illustrations in medical texts and natural histories. There was talk of Ernest's becoming a doctor, and his father beamed when the boy signed himself "Ernest M. Hemingway, M.D.," in a guest register.

Winter brought special pleasures. For one thing, Oak Park got a lot of snow. Ernest and Marcelline left the house early on snowy mornings and spent hours hurtling down hills on sleds, tossing snowballs, and building fortresses and snowmen.

And, of course, winter brought Christmas. During the weeks before the holiday the children helped their father in the preparation of exotic and highly spiced delicacies. Dr. Hemingway led the children to the large fruit cellar where they joined him in rubbing seasonings into roasts of beef or into boiled and flavored ham hocks, or checked on the progress of the quarts of pickles the doctor put up each year. And then there were the excitement of wrapping presents for others, the impatience of waiting to open their own gifts, and—finally—the delights of Christmas Day.

But all of Oak Park's diversions and attractions were little more for Ernest than ways of passing time until summer. He endured the necessity of education, dutifully sat over the piano keyboard, and joined in snowball fights, but his thoughts remained in Michigan at Walloon Lake. It was in the big woods that he was most at home.

Each summer at Walloon he felt more comfortable, more a part of nature. It seemed that he wanted to strip himself of every unpleasant responsibility imposed by city life. During Ernest's eighth summer, 1907, he removed his shoes the moment he reached the beach at Windemere and did not put them on again until it was time to return to Oak Park. He did not need shoes:

the soles of his feet grew thick and tough with calluses. When his father gathered the family for the return home, Ernest dressed in his city clothes but did not put on his shoes. Dr. Hemingway would have none of that; no child of his would appear in public barefoot. Ernest struggled to squeeze his feet into his shoes. He had grown during the summer, and when he finally forced the shoes on they were so tight, and hurt so much, that Ernest could walk only slowly and with a limp. Dr. Hemingway was sympathetic but inflexible: in public Ernest must wear shoes.

As the family moved toward the train in Harbor Springs, a stranger drew Ernest aside and gave him a shiny dime. Along with the coin the man expressed his sadness that so handsome a young boy was so badly crippled. Fortunately, Dr. Hemingway found the incident amusing, and the whole family laughed about it. Ernest got new shoes at the next stop.

While Dr. Hemingway was pleased with Ernest's interest in the natural world, he was less than thrilled with his son's schoolwork. Ernest had great trouble with mathematics, and the doctor insisted that the boy spend long hours at his books. Math texts, though, were hardly the sorts of books Ernest found exciting. He liked novels and stories. His father did not approve. The doctor tried repeatedly to convince Ernest that such reading material only wasted time. He held particular disdain for novels; he could see little purpose or improvement to be gained by reading fiction.

There were some exceptions. *John Halifax, Gentleman,* by Dinah Maria Mulock, was one novel the doctor admired without reservation. Originally published in 1856, *John Halifax, Gentleman* was a didactic novel—a novel with a message. It taught that no matter what tragedies life presented, they could be overcome by discipline, a positive attitude, and unwavering faith in God. Poverty, illness, financial crisis, death—all are faced foursquare by John Halifax, whose moral courage and pious optimism cannot be dimmed. Dr. Hemingway, who shared those values, recommended Mrs. Mulock's novel to anyone looking for uplifting reading. When treating young people, the doctor often presented them with a copy of the novel, and urged his patients' parents to read the book along with their children.

While Ernest read the novel—all of the children read it, and Ursula's name was derived from one of its characters, as was Longfield Farm, which was one of the book's settings—he was not so taken by it as was his father. Its characters were too impossibly good. Ernest could not believe in passages such as the one in which, after a violent food riot, the narrator describes for the hundredth time John Halifax's goodness: "He was life and health to me, with his brave cheerfulness—his way of turning all minor trouble into pleasantries, till they seemed to break and vanish away, sparkling, like the foam on the top of the wave. Yet, all the while, one knew well that he could meet any great evil as gallantly as a good ship meets a heavy sea—breasting it, plunging through it, as only a good ship can."

Ernest liked tales of triumph, but he demanded more realism than Mrs. Mulock's novel offered. He preferred books in which heroes won by their toughness, their fearlessness, and their fists, rather than by simple belief in Christian virtue. He was addicted to Horatio Alger's rags-to-riches stories. Another favorite was Daniel Defoe's *Robinson Crusoe,* which his father gave him one Christmas. Sir Walter Scott's *Ivanhoe* was another permitted novel that Ernest enjoyed.

Ernest learned quickly that he could read whatever he wanted to, so long as he kept proscribed titles out of his father's sight. The boy became adept at hiding forbidden works, indulging his growing taste for books that offered glimpses of worlds and attitudes far removed from comfortable, quiet Oak Park. A particular favorite was Robert Louis Stevenson's *The Suicide Club,* which Ernest found, oddly enough, on his father's shelves. *The Suicide Club* was exciting and dramatic, wonderfully well written without the florid overwriting that characterized so many of the Victorian novels his father allowed.

Stevenson's story led Ernest into the depths of London, into a world of vice and dissipation and decadence, introducing him to characters so filled with despair or boredom that they sought suicide. A villain, host of the Suicide Club, provided deaths for his guests. Justice did, in a way, triumph in the story, but it was not the justice of God or even of law—it was the justice of a single man who deemed himself judge and executioner, taking moral action as he saw fit. Ernest loved the story, and read it repeatedly.

Other books—more refined and less immediately reward-ing—were on Dr. Hemingway's mind. Ernest's grades were be-coming an embarrassment, and in fact were threatening his fu-ture. In the spring of 1908 the doctor was informed that unless Ernest greatly improved his mathematical skills during the sum-mer, he would not be promoted to fourth grade in the fall. The family still hoped that Ernest would become a physician, but the doctor knew that the groundwork for a medical career must be laid now. Otherwise Ernest's hopes of adding an M.D. to his name would never be realized. Dr. Hemingway had faith in Ernest's intelligence, but he could find no way to persuade the boy to bring more concentration to his studies.

That summer at Windemere, Dr. Hemingway grew stern in his insistence that Ernest master his schoolwork. Regular study of math was added to Ernest's other chores. It was a task that Ernest greeted without enthusiasm and that he avoided more often than undertook. His mind was on other, more important things, especially a three-day fishing trip his father was plan-ning.

Dr. Hemingway was adamant. Ernest would not be per-mitted on the trip unless he could prove his mastery of the required math. In order to earn his promotion Ernest had to know completely the multiplication tables through twelve. The doctor's ultimatum was accompanied by a requirement: if Er-nest wanted to go on the trip, he had to pass a test in multiplica-tion. And since Ernest had lately complained about canned beans, which would be the trip's basic bill of fare, Dr. Hemingway added another demand: Ernest must eat an entire large can of beans along with learning multiplication. Only if he accomplished both things could he go fishing.

It struck Ernest as an impossible order. Mathematics could not capture his attention, and the beans caught in his throat. Tomorrow, he said, making the easiest of promises—he would eat beans and study tomorrow.

Only as the fishing trip neared did Ernest begin to take his responsibilities more seriously. The prospect of missing the season's longest expedition was unthinkable. He could not miss it. He would not miss it. Six times five, Ernest said to himself with increasing determination, six times six. Marcelline helped him with the tables, calling out a problem and correcting him when he gave an incorrect answer. Ernest objected when Marcelline broke the sequence of the tables, but his sister knew their father well: Dr. Hemingway's test would be random, and so was her tutoring.

The numbers danced and shimmered, their pattern sometimes clear, more often obscure. Ernest kept at it. He gave up such pleasures as swimming and hiking, did his chores quickly and efficiently, earning more time for study. With each meal and frequently in between meals, he ate several spoonfuls of canned beans, forcing himself to smile as he chewed and swallowed. He wanted to accompany his father on the fishing trip; he wanted to prove that he was up to the challenge his father set for him.

Finally he scraped the last taste of beans from the bottom of the can, and finally he faced his father for a test on the multiplication tables. Dr. Hemingway smiled with relief and pride— Ernest succeeded at both assignments. He congratulated his son and pointed out what they both had known all along—Ernest could accomplish anything he set his mind to. He was an exceptionally intelligent boy. There was no limit, the doctor said, to what could be done in life if Ernest would only remember the lessons he'd learned. Discipline, concentration, hard work—

words that had been repeated to Ernest far more often than the tables of multiplication—perhaps now Ernest had truly learned their meaning.

The fishing trip was a great success and Ernest's skills with a rod were much in evidence. He was patient, he concentrated, he had more than enough discipline to wait until the precise moment to set the hook in a fish's mouth. Dr. Hemingway used the long hours in the boat, exploring coves and the streams that flowed into Walloon Lake, to talk with Ernest. The talent that made the boy such a fine fisherman could also be harnessed in service to learning, said the doctor. And once harnessed, Ernest's energy and intelligence would make him a gifted and successful physician.

In the fall Ernest entered fourth grade. Soon his marks began to slip once more; once more he revealed his boredom, his lack of discipline. One lesson had been acquired, though. While mathematics would always give him trouble, Ernest for the rest of his life retained a fondness for the taste of canned beans.

THREE

ADVENTURES

IF HE EXPERIENCED GREAT DIFFICULTY manipulating numbers, Ernest enjoyed exactly the opposite relationship with words. He loved to play with words, toy with them, make puns and savor sounds, juggle a rhyme or utter a snappy piece of slang. Words came alive for him not just on the pages of books, but also in his conversation. He tried to find new and original ways of saying things, always avoiding the clichéd, trite, or dull. English was the one subject that never gave him difficulty.

He took great delight in concocting nicknames for his sisters. For years he referred to Marcelline as Masween or Mash, but after seeing a play he christened her "The Great Iverian" in mocking reference to one of its characters. Later he shortened this to Ivory. When she was young, Ursula was "Mrs. Giggs" or just Giggs. The nickname Sunny, assigned to Madelaine as an infant, lingered with her throughout her life.

Ernest played with his own name as well. As a toddler he called himself Pawnee Bill. He also answered to "Chipmunk." When he grew older, he enjoyed slurring *Ern* into *Oin*, which later became "Oinbones." He proclaimed himself Ernest Oinbones, man of courage, and said that this was a fit name for any hero.

He was becoming his own hero, patterning his actions after those he read about in books, newspapers, and magazines. His fascination with boxing did not fade, and he memorized facts about the sport, as well as mimicking famous boxers' stances.

Another hero lived closer to home. Ernest's great-uncle Tyley Hancock, Grace's uncle, was a traveling salesman who often stayed with the Hemingways, both in Oak Park and at Walloon Lake. As a boy Tyley Hancock had sailed around the world three times. Ernest never tired of sitting and listening to Uncle Tyley's stories of far places and strange sights. Ernest heard the stories so often he could recite them by heart.

When not telling stories, Uncle Tyley taught Ernest how to fly-fish. Tyley Hancock was an even better fisherman than Dr. Hemingway, and under his tutelage Ernest soon learned to tie his own flies, cast them gracefully, and manipulate them on the water as though they were alive. Their best times were when Tyley would visit Walloon Lake and he and Ernest would sneak off in search of trout. Tyley thought Ernest was a natural fisherman, gifted with all the instincts. He said Ernest even thought like a fish.

Ernest thought like his heroes. He believed what they believed, and though he outgrew the heroes of his childhood, scraps of their attitudes clung to him. He possessed a bit of the boxer's code of fairness, the cowboy's resourcefulness, some of Robinson Crusoe and Ivanhoe, large pieces of his father and Uncle Tyley, even a trace of John Halifax.

The largest share of Ernest's admiration, though, was reserved for his father. There was nothing Clarence Hemingway could not accomplish. Ernest watched as his father carefully built a campfire, as his strong surgeon's hands deftly controlled a knife as he cleaned a fish, and as his father expertly cooked the catch.

Best of all was watching Dr. Hemingway shoot. Ernest knew even as a boy that he would never be as fine a shot as his father. Dr. Hemingway never missed, no matter how distant or swiftly moving his target. He knew some tricks, too, and he shared those with his son. One afternoon at Windemere the doctor put on a shooting exhibition for Ernest and some visitors. Dr. Hemingway announced that he would shoot a candle through a one-inch board. Everyone laughed: such a feat was clearly impossible.

Dr. Hemingway said nothing more. The guests teased him as he set up his board. He had already removed the shot from a cartridge and now he replaced it with a piece of wax candle. He took aim at the board and fired. As he promised, the candle passed completely through the board, leaving a perfectly circular hole, just as a bullet would. No one else could do it. Others tried, but their candles left only grease spots on the board.

Later he called Ernest aside and told him how the trick was accomplished. It was easy to do, provided your candle was completely frozen, making it as hard as a bullet. When he let the others in on the joke he made them, and Ernest, promise never to use the gag for money. Dr. Hemingway had accepted no wagers against his claim, and neither should they. Gambling on chance alone was a sin, but gambling on such a trick was worse. Ernest nodded solemnly and made the promise.

Although it was becoming increasingly obvious that Ernest's prospects for a medical career were limited, the boy still watched with enjoyment his father's practice of medicine. He accompanied Dr. Hemingway on his visits to the Indian camp near Windemere, and observed with interest as his father treated the lumbermen and their families. Ernest noticed the difference between his proper, gentlemanly father and the rough men who felled the trees. It was quite a contrast and Ernest gave it a good deal of thought.

Even as Ernest's grades were slipping, Dr. Hemingway continued to study and improve his own skills. He spent four months one summer studying new techniques in obstetrics. Delivering babies was one of the doctor's specialties, and the family celebrated when he delivered his thousandth child, and then when he reached two thousand. Before his career ended, Dr. Hemingway delivered more than three thousand babies.

More than once the doctor was called upon to treat his own children. Most often the child in need of treatment was Ernest.

The boy's awkwardness and lack of grace made him accident-prone. Once, running through the woods near Windemere, a stick cocked in his mouth like a cigar, Ernest stumbled and fell, driving the stick into the back of his throat, gouging out part of each tonsil and loosing a torrent of blood. He ran home as fast as he could, nearly choking on the blood, spitting out what seemed like quarts of it. Grace screamed when she saw her son, but Dr. Hemingway remained calm. He quieted Ernest, stopped the hemorrhaging, and sterilized the wound. He placed Ernest on a rich diet to replace the blood he'd lost. And when Ernest complained of soreness in his throat, his father told him to ignore the pain and whistle a cheerful tune instead; whistling was better than any painkiller.

Clarence Hemingway believed it was important for a man to develop a tolerance for pain. He told stories of his own stoicism, and stories of times when, though stoicism failed him, he remained in control of his emotions. On one fishing trip, he said, he developed blood poisoning as a result of a hook that became embedded in his left arm. The arm grew swollen, thick with fluids and pus. The nearest community was some distance away, and for once he did not have his medical bag with him. The arm must be drained before gangrene set in, and no one among the doctor's companions had any medical training. He decided to lance the arm himself, and heated his knife until it glowed red. The other men held him while Dr. Hemingway took a deep breath and opened his arm with the knife. The release of pressure caused pus to spurt several feet, and the pain tore a powerful scream from the doctor. He admitted he wept from the pain, but he made the more important point: he had not been afraid to face agony when it was necessary.

Ernest respected that attitude toward pain immensely, and he grew increasingly unwilling to admit any discomfort. Ernest would not fail to live up to the standards his father set.

In other ways the differences between father and son became more pronounced each year. Ernest's interest in the rougher aspects of life—which he encountered almost exclusively through reading—provoked more than one confrontation. Dr. Hemingway might on occasion look the other way when Ernest wanted to read Robert Louis Stevenson, but the boy was beginning to seek books that were unequivocally forbidden. Ernest took great pleasure in smuggling the works of Jack London and other proscribed authors into his home. In such books he found little evidence of the value of virtue, the importance of social standing and propriety. Ernest loved stories in which triumph was less important than survival, and survival belonged to those who were willing to fight harder, who were stronger and sometimes less ethical than those with whom they were in conflict. Strength and fearlessness were the keys to survival, and the goal was to be tougher than the other guy.

The more he read, the more interested Ernest became in writing stories of his own. In the sixth grade in 1911 he tried his hand at a short story. He called it "My First Sea Vouge," revealing—not for the last time—his difficulty with spelling. The entire brief tale was concocted from his Uncle Tyley's reminiscences. Only a few paragraphs long, "My First Sea Vouge" told in the first person the story of a voyage by sailing ship from "Massachuset" to Australia, with descriptions of the birds and animals spotted along the way.

Ernest's first short story was not much of a story, but it revealed the close attention the boy had paid to his uncle's yarns. Ernest was already a close observer of the world around him, and as he grew older he became aware that the relationships between people could be as fascinating and instructive to watch as the workings of nature.

He began to see more deeply into his parents' marriage. They were by all the evidence a successful couple, prominent members of Oak Park society. Their social position was important to Grace, and when her husband daydreamed aloud of moving the family to a practice in the West, or of becoming a missionary like his brother Will, Grace quickly stopped such talk.

Doctor Hemingway's career in Oak Park was too well established, too important. He served as head of obstetrics at an Oak Park hospital, as medical examiner for three insurance companies, and as medical examiner for the Borden Milk Company. To think of leaving Oak Park was foolish. They had a life there, a life they had built together.

Mornings began with breakfast in bed for Grace, prepared and delivered by her husband. Before school the family gathered for prayer, Bible reading, and hymns. Religion was a focus of the family's life, and in addition to church they often attended tent revivals. At one such revival Ernest sat motionless in his seat after everyone in his family and everyone else in the tent had gone forth to witness. The evangelist called out again and again for all who waited to stand and come forward. At last Ernest joined the others. He'd hesitated so long, he said, in order to test the preacher's endurance.

Equal to religion in Grace's order of values was high culture, particularly music. She wanted each of her children not only to be exposed to the arts, but also to develop their own artistic gifts to the fullest. She often told her daughters of the great career as an opera singer she could have had. Their mother, she assured them, would have been celebrated worldwide for her musical gift. Grace sought to pass that gift on to her offspring, giving each of them piano lessons and enrolling them in courses of instruction for other instruments. Ernest, against his will, spent many hours in cello lessons and practice. He did not display much talent for music, but Grace was thrilled when, for a few weeks during puberty, her son's voice was a perfect soprano.

The huge music room remained the center of Grace's life, and she hoped someday to add a pipe organ to the collection of instruments. Ernest loved the room as well, but for different reasons. Its size made it possible to clear a large central area of the floor, an area large enough to be used as a boxing ring. When his mother was away from home Ernest would invite his friends over for sparring practice, taking care to hide all the evidence when practice was done. These matches were serious business for Ernest, and he insisted that all the details and rituals of the sport be observed. There were a water pail and towels, a referee, and neutral corners. Ernest frequently enlisted Sunny to serve as timekeeper for the sessions.

The early months of 1911 found Grace pregnant again, and as always the house buzzed with the hope that there would be another boy in the family. When the baby was born on July 19, though, it was a girl, who was named Carol. Ernest's disappointment at not getting a brother may have been eased by the shotgun he received as a twelfth-birthday present.

He carried the gun everywhere. It was a sign of approaching manhood, and Ernest was impatient to become a man. Each summer at Walloon Lake he showed more independence, revealed a stronger desire to be on his own, away from the family. His love for northern Michigan did not diminish, but his willingness to be confined to Windemere and the tame yard around the cabin decreased daily. Dr. and Mrs. Hemingway, in keeping with their intentions to show their children the finer things in life, as well as to improve their public manners, often took the family by rowboat across the lake for dinner at one of the fashionable resort hotels on the shorefront. They saw finely dressed gentlemen and ladies, a sight that bored Ernest and reminded him of everything he hoped to escape. At the hotels they ate from china plates, but Ernest preferred to join the communal meals at the Indian camp near the cabin.

The Indians became his friends, and Ernest often passed his free time at the logging camp. The older loggers, fearful that the boy would be injured, often sent him home, but Ernest always returned. He grew especially close to Dick and Prudence Boulton, whose father, Nick, was one of the loggers. On long walks through the Michigan woods Ernest and Dick compared ideas about hunting and fishing. Ernest and Prudence flirted with each other, and Ernest asked what it was like to live in a shack: there were no shacks back in Oak Park. When deadhead logs washed onto the beach at Windemere, Ernest's father hired Indians to saw them into firewood, although the logs were still considered the property of the lumber company.

Other work at Walloon Lake was accomplished by the Hemingway children, and as he grew older Ernest was assigned more responsibility. He gathered ice from the supply stored under sawdust in the family icehouse. Every morning the beach had to be raked clean. Longfield Farm across the lake demanded increasing attention. Dr. Hemingway planted potatoes, straw- berries, truck vegetables, and hay, although he always main- tained that the best thing raised at the farm was the flag. Ernest and his sisters spent long hours stooped over the crops, plucking insects from them and dropping the pests into cans.

The old debate about barefootedness resumed when Dr. Hemingway found Ernest chopping wood while shoeless. The boy was skilled with the axe, wielding it in long, even arcs, proud of his muscles. But, as his father pointed out, he'd just treated a boy who'd nearly amputated a foot by working so foolishly. Ernest wore shoes from that point on.

The summer of 1913 was an especially important one for Ernest. In the fall he would enter high school, another sign that childhood was nearly over. So was family life, at least as far as Ernest was concerned that summer. He wanted further to estab- lish his independence, and soon after arriving at the lake he moved out of Windemere and into a small tent behind the cot- tage.

He loved the isolation and privacy. In his tent he could do anything, be anything. There was no one to tuck him in as a child might be tucked in, no one to insist that his lantern be extinguished. He could stay up all night if he wanted to, and his light burned late and long as Ernest squinted over a book.

The children were allowed, before leaving Oak Park, to visit the public library and check out a summer's worth of read- ing. Dr. Hemingway made it clear that the children were responsible for the care of the books they withdrew and for paying their own fines if any of their books were damaged or lost. They took this charge seriously and the books were returned in excellent condition.

Just as they had differed over the necessity of shoes, Ernest and his father disagreed about the boy's reading. They disputed not simply the subject matter Ernest selected, but also the amount of reading he did. He could not get enough, burying himself in books for hours, clutching a new volume as soon as an old one was completed. He appreciated the difference in approach taken by various authors, relished the ways in which writers used language, and thrilled to exciting stories. His father constantly admonished him to get his nose out of the books, to put his hands to work at something more constructive than turning the pages of worthless novels.

One night the family was awakened by loud cries of terror from Ernest's tent. They rushed outside, fully expecting to find a snake or animal or perhaps a prowler. The truth was immediately clear. Beside Ernest was the book he'd been reading, Bram Stoker's *Dracula*. The tent had been invaded by nightmare vampires; the terrors came from Ernest's imagination. Dr. Hemingway showed his disdain clearly and returned to the house.

When Ernest was discovered reading rather than doing his work at Longfield Farm, the doctor had had enough. He issued a firm order: Ernest was not to be allowed to read. The family was instructed to keep books away from Ernest, and the help was told to take books from the boy's hands by force if necessary. The only reading material Ernest was permitted was the *Journal of the American Medical Association,* which at least would help prepare Ernest for the medical career his father still planned for him.

Each morning Ernest set out for Longfield Farm with his tools and his lunch. There was no point in trying to smuggle books along—they would be discovered and the situation would worsen. The problem seemed to be under control, the doctor thought, until he visited the farm during working hours and found his son beneath a tree, avidly reading the boxing results from the tattered piece of newspaper in which his lunch had been wrapped.

When not working, or working out schemes by which to read, Ernest prowled through the woods in search of game. Dr. Hemingway had made it clear to Ernest that nothing was to be shot other than for food, but Ernest occasionally violated that rule. When vacationers pitched camp on Indian Point, one of Ernest's favorite spots, he shot a skunk and buried it in the sand. The odor soon drove the campers away.

Thanks to his father's tutelage, he was quite a good shot. The summer before, Ernest had killed enough pigeons to make a fine pie, and while carrying the birds home he was asked by some older boys who had bagged the birds. Ernest replied proudly that he had. The boys laughed at him and Ernest, well practiced from the boxing sessions in the music room, began to fight. He was soundly beaten but would not deny the truth. He'd killed the birds with his own gun, with his own skill. He would not back down and he would not show fear.

Now, the summer before high school, Ernest was fourteen and eager to display his fearlessness. His most frequent audience was his sister Sunny. When she warned him of nearby poison ivy Ernest smiled broadly, plucked a handful of leaves, and cheerfully chewed and swallowed them while Sunny squealed. Later, when he stepped on a rusty nail, he insisted that Sunny suck the blood from the wound to prevent tetanus. He did not complain or grimace.

Ernest and Sunny were constant companions, and now that the family owned two boats—one of them powered—he sometimes took the girl with him on fishing trips. He showed her how to sneak up on trout, how to bait a hook, how to be quiet enough to fool the fish into complacency. And always he demonstrated his personal courage. On one trip Sunny accidentally hooked

Ernest in the back. The hook was well embedded and could not easily be removed. Both Ernest and his sister recalled their father's story of the blood poisoning that resulted from being hooked. Ernest gave Sunny his knife and insisted that she cut the hook out. But she would not—could not—and they returned to Windemere, where Ernest was treated by his father.

Heroism was important to Ernest. It was part of courage. A hero had to be ready to respond immediately to any challenge, to face problems without fear or hesitation. Because his father had to spend much of the summer in Oak Park tending to his practice, Ernest served as the man of the family, and he searched for ways to prove his manhood. He was reading in his tent one night when he smelled smoke and looked up to see flames in Sunny's bedroom in the cabin. He did not hesitate but rushed into the house, woke the family and sent them outside while he extinguished the fire. A candle had been brushed by the curtains, and the fire was easily contained. It could have been much worse, though, and Sunny's already deep hero worship grew stronger.

A hero, his father could have told Ernest, needs to react quickly but does not always react without thinking. Ernest and a friend were hunting one afternoon when the friend's dog encountered a porcupine and emerged from the confrontation with sharp quills embedded in its nose. Ernest tracked down the porcupine and shot it, then proudly carried the evidence of his prowess back to Windemere. His father was not impressed. The porcupine had done nothing wrong; it had only been defending itself against an unwanted intruder. Ernest had wasted a life. Dr. Hemingway insisted that Ernest and his friend dress the porcupine, cook it, and eat it. They cooked it for hours, to no avail. The meat was tough and oily, but every bit of it was eventually consumed.

As the summer drew to a close, Ernest did not feel the melancholy that customarily overcame him as he returned to Oak Park. This fall was different. He and Marcelline would enter high school, and he at last would be considered a young man. The only regret he experienced was over his height: at fourteen he stood only five feet four inches, the shortest boy in his class.

He did not have too much time to agonize over his stature. Oak Park High School was one of the toughest in Illinois, with more than two-thirds of each graduating class going on to college, and a large number of those earning scholarships. Ernest's freshman curriculum included algebra, English, Latin (in which he had to be tutored), general science, biology, ensemble, gymnastics, and manual training. Despite his excitement about high school, Ernest's attitude toward education had not improved. He applied himself to English and the other subjects that interested him, and ignored the others.

Gradually the family surrendered the last traces of hope for a medical career for Ernest. He did not have the necessary discipline; his science and mathematics grades were poor. The only high mark he earned in a science class was for a paper on the anatomy of the grasshopper. It was a masterful paper, complete and accurate. That paper was easy for Ernest—he had studied grasshoppers for years. They made wonderful bait.

His freshman English course at least gave him the opportunity to read. The class made its way through *Idylls of the King,* by Alfred, Lord Tennyson; *The Rime of the Ancient Mariner,* by Samuel Coleridge; a volume of ballads in Old English; Scott's *Ivanhoe,* which Ernest had already read; and Benjamin Franklin's *Autobiography.* Perhaps most important was the study of the Bible, with emphasis on the narrative style employed in each book. In addition, there was a little outside reading, including some contemporary writers—but not too much. Like Clarence Hemingway, Frank Platt, the English teacher, found contemporary writers unimproving and unnecessary.

When he was not studying, Ernest spent his afternoons working. Oak Park offered more opportunity for a boy to earn pocket money than did Walloon Lake, and Ernest hired himself out for a variety of chores. In autumn and spring he mowed lawns; during the winter months he shoveled snow. He served as a neighborhood delivery boy for *Oak Leaves,* a local weekly, and that task took several hours each publication day. While Dr. Hemingway encouraged the boy's self-reliance, he could be sympathetically helpful. On those occasions when a particularly thick issue of *Oak Leaves* appeared, father and son delivered the papers together, riding in the doctor's car.

Free time was spent with friends. Ernest's locker at Oak Park High School was flanked by the lockers of his two best friends; they adorned the doors with yellow circles, so that the cluster came to be known as the Three Ball Joint. They met between classes and after school to plan adventures that included weekend hunting expeditions to the still-wild countryside surrounding Oak Park. Occasionally they would indoctrinate another young man into their society, taking him at night to Ernest's darkened bedroom, where mumbo jumbo was uttered and an initiation performed. Part of the initiation involved rubbing the blindfolded pledge with the skin of a porcupine. Dr. and Mrs. Hemingway ignored the screams that came from their son's room during initiation.

Freshman year came to an end, and the summer of 1914 was spent, as always, at Walloon Lake. Ernest took along a friend, and they lived in a tent at Longfield Farm, working the crops with more dedication than Ernest had previously shown. He wanted the exercise; he wanted to be tough. That summer Ernest began to grow, gaining as much as an inch of height a month, his frame filling out, losing his childish appearance. He had thought of himself as a young man for some time, and now he looked like one. His parents could not pretend any longer that Ernest was still a child. In the fall, when he entered his sophomore year, he was allowed for the first time to wear long pants rather than knickers.

Clarence and Grace Hemingway were also becoming aware that Ernest would set his own direction in life. They had attempted as best they could to guide him and provide for him opportunities from which he could build a successful academic and then professional career. Ernest had not risen to those opportunities, and privately the Hemingways felt that he would have to make his own luck. They could do no more than they had done.

Ernest proceeded, blithely cheerful, confident of his own abilities and ambitions, however unfocused they might be. He was sixteen years old and could do whatever he wanted. His days of bending over a cello or memorizing multiplication tables were drawing to a close. His love of reading remained strong and his interest in writing grew stronger. Always cocky, he already bragged that he was a better writer than Cicero. Perhaps he would make his living with a pen.

That was for the future, though, and the present saw more changes than just his appearance. Ernest attended the opera in Chicago, riding in on the elevated train with his sister Marcelline. Grace was delighted to learn that her son was moved to tears by Butterfly's death at the end of *Madama Butterfly*. She would have been less thrilled to learn that Ernest on other days took the elevated to less cultured areas of Chicago, where he hung around training gymnasiums, watching fighters and their managers prepare for bouts. This, he thought, was his world.

Autumn 1914 brought the news that Grace was pregnant. Everyone assumed that this would be her last child, and the hope was deeper than ever that she would have another boy. Ernest realized that, whether boy or girl, the new child would be more like a cousin than a sibling. Ernest would be leaving home soon, for college or work. Or perhaps the army—war had erupted in Europe, and although the United States was not involved, Ernest followed the news reports avidly.

He was also beginning to pay attention to girls. On several occasions he accompanied Marcelline to parties, and finally worked up the courage to ask a schoolmate for a date. She accepted and Ernest took her to a basketball game. He enjoyed himself, but no romance developed. He was not ready for that yet.

On April 1, 1915, Grace delivered her last child, the long-awaited second boy. He was named Leicester (pronounced *Lester*) Clarence Hemingway, but Ernest soon issued the infant a nickname. Leicester De Pester, he called him, and even composed a bit of doggerel in the baby's honor: "Leicester Clarence/pesters parents."

When summer 1915 arrived, Ernest and a pal were allowed to make the journey to Walloon Lake ahead of the family and deal with the work involved in making the cabin and grounds ready for summer. The boys set up a tent and divided their time between chores and trout fishing. After the family's arrival, Ernest remained in his tent at Longfield Farm.

Dr. Hemingway was away from Walloon Lake a good part of the summer, and Ernest took even more strongly to the role of man of the family, protector. He was eager to prove his maturity, just as he was eager to demonstrate his hunting prowess. Ernest paid attention to his sisters, especially Sunny, and let them accompany him on expeditions from time to time.

One afternoon he and Sunny were in a boat making their way across the lake when a startled blue heron took to the air. Almost instinctively Ernest slapped his shotgun up, followed the bird, and brought it down. Not only had he violated his father's code of not killing simply for pleasure, he had broken the law. Blue herons were a protected species.

Ernest carelessly left the dead bird in the launch and it was discovered and the game warden notified. The warden came to Windemere and confronted Grace, telling her of Ernest's crime, but doing so rudely. Grace drew herself to her full height, stepped into the cottage, and reappeared with a shotgun. She would not tolerate such behavior, no matter what Ernest had done. The warden retreated, but the matter was not yet settled.

Frightened, but at the same time playing the role of the fugitive well, Ernest fled to a relative's home some distance away. He went into hiding and returned to Walloon Lake only at night to pick vegetables and gather food for his family. Finally Dr. Hemingway, who had been notified, wrote and advised Ernest to appear in court and settle the matter. Ernest received a lecture and a fifteen-dollar fine. He had quite a story to tell when he returned to school.

His junior year was the most challenging yet, with Ernest studying English, Latin, ancient history, chemistry, and music, and playing—though not well—on the football team. Chicago's gymnasiums called to him more frequently, and his interest in boxing showed no sign of fading. He took the sport seriously, and worked out on a regular schedule.

During his junior year he also began applying himself more seriously and with greater regularity to writing. One of his courses involved writing essays, but Ernest was also beginning to write short stories. In February 1916, the school literary magazine, the *Tabula,* printed a 700-word short story by Ernest Hemingway. The story was called "The Judgment of Manitou" and dealt with Indians, revenge, and death in the woods. In April Ernest published in the magazine another story, "A Matter of Colour," which was a humorous tale of boxers and the world in which they lived. He was beginning to test his skills at reproducing on paper the material he observed in life.

He also worked on the *Trapeze,* Oak Park High School's newspaper. The *Trapeze* appeared every week, and between January 1916 and May 1917, when he graduated, Ernest's by-line appeared over more than thirty stories. At first his pieces were simple pieces on sporting events or school organizations, but gradually Ernest became more ambitious. He wrote a long story about a friend's heroism. He experimented with humor and with different voices for his stories; he used dialogue. He began to speak of journalism as a career.

Early in the summer after his junior year he and a friend set out on their most extended camping trip yet. They hiked through wild territory, discovering trout streams, enjoying feeling rugged and rough. Ernest put the lie to his outdoorsman's appearance, however, by making constant entries in a notebook. He was recording his observations systematically, writing out ideas for short stories and articles, testing his powers of description against the land as he encountered it.

At last his senior year began. High school would soon lie behind him, and Ernest was more certain than ever that his future lay in journalism. He enrolled in elective courses, the most difficult of which was English VI. That class modeled itself after a newspaper office, with students receiving a different assignment each day. Every aspect of newspaper work was covered in the class, from editorial writing to advertising writing and layout, reporting to proofreading, headlines to personal columns. It was the most wonderful course of Ernest's high school career.

Increasingly he was drawn to the writing of personal columns, and increasingly the model he used for his columns was Ring Lardner, whose columns for the *Chicago Tribune* were among the most popular and famous in the nation. Lardner's columns were humorous, using to great effect dialect voices captured perfectly by Lardner's ear. Beneath the humor, and clear in the subjects' voices, were genuine human feelings, including pain and fear. The columns had a profound effect upon other columnists and fiction writers of the period, and they are still read today.

Ernest studied Lardner closely and put what he learned to work in the pages of the *Trapeze*. His columns were light, dealing with gossip and the tribulations of adolescence, often cast as conversations or letters to classmates. He addressed personal messages to Marcelline, joked about his fishing and hunting companions, and even made fun of the form in which he worked, explaining that one column was so wordy because he had a set amount of space to fill.

Just as Ring Lardner's pieces seemed shocking to many staid readers, Ernest's imitations caused some concern and provoked some disapproval in the high school's administrative offices. The columns by the Hemingway boy, they felt, verged upon the scandalous, and there were suggestions from the principal's office that Ernest be instructed to use more discretion in his choice of subject matter and more judgment in the tone he selected for its presentation.

Ernest pressed on undeterred. Each new column was more outrageous than the one that preceded it. He began to include bragging references to heavy drinking and carousing, most of it imaginary and all of it deliberately inflammatory. Ernest enjoyed the controversy. He had discovered early the pleasure he derived from violating conventions.

He also enjoyed the popularity the columns earned him among his peers. He did not earn athletic distinction at Oak Park High School—he was not good at football, and he won his athletic letter for service as manager of the track team. Ernest's prestige came from his columns, from the bright and original way he used words.

In addition to reporting, Ernest continued to work at fiction. The November 1916 *Tabula* held another short story by Ernest Hemingway. "Sepi Jingan" was another story of the woods, of Indians and murder. Ernest used the name of one of the Indians he knew at Walloon Lake, Billy Tabeshaw, for a character in the story.

It would take time, Ernest knew, for him to be able to earn a living writing fiction. But he could make a living as a reporter, and work on his fiction at the same time. Besides, reporters encountered the truth of life as they worked. They saw areas of the world, types of people, and incidents unimaginable in Oak Park. It would be a wonderful way to gather experience in life as well as in writing.

As his June graduation neared, Ernest continued to write fiction. He turned in weekly stories for the *Trapeze* and worked on the Class Prophecy he was to deliver. Somehow he also managed to schedule a weekend camping trip with some friends. Deep in the woods, in the middle of the night, they were set upon by a gang. Ernest threw an axe at the head of one of the attackers and luckily missed—they were boys from Oak

Park High, playing a prank. Ernest wrote a piece about the attack for the *Trapeze.*

The *Trapeze* also mentioned his plans to study journalism as a fall freshman at the University of Illinois, but that story was inaccurate. Although Marcelline would enter Oberlin College in the fall, Ernest's formal education ended with his high school graduation. He had no intention of going to college, and through the early weeks of summer, relations between Ernest and his father grew strained. The doctor attempted repeatedly to make Ernest see how foolish he was being, but Ernest would not listen. He was impatient to be away from home, to be on his own. More than once, after harsh words from his father, Ernest hid in a shed and with an empty shotgun took careful aim at his father's head.

Gradually, Dr. Hemingway relented. He was not going to change Ernest. The boy would have to find his own way, although the doctor wanted to help in any way he could. He had a few contacts and attempted to secure Ernest a position on the *Kansas City Star.*

As they waited for word about the job, the summer of 1917 went by. Ernest got in plenty of fishing and hunting, and worked the fields at Longfield Farm. He built a new icehouse for Windemere. He also followed carefully the news of World War I, which the United States had entered in April. War would be a bigger adventure than work, but Ernest had been turned down by the armed services because of his poor eyesight. He continued to hope, however, to find a way to get overseas. He watched as mobilized young men marched by; he laughed at his mother's hoarding of canned lobster and shrimp against the deprivations of war. He dreamed of action.

Finally, word arrived from the *Kansas City Star.* Ernest would join the staff in October. He could not contain himself. A reporter! He would be seeing a new part of the world, and seeing it with the eyes of a professional newsman. He would be on his way.

┌ FOUR ┐

REPORTER

WHEN ERNEST AND HIS FATHER said good-bye at the railroad station in October, his father began to cry. Ernest was embarrassed and at the same time must have felt shame over the anger he'd revealed during the summer. His father only wanted the best for him; how could Ernest have dreamed of killing him? Now father and son embraced and the doctor wished Ernest well. There would be some ties: at least initially Ernest would be living with his uncle Tyler Hemingway. Dr. Hemingway took comfort in that, although he suspected that Ernest's stay with Tyler would be temporary. Ernest was too independent to linger long at his uncle's home.

The train pulled out of the station and Ernest watched his father for a while, then lost sight of him and turned his eyes ahead, toward the adventure that awaited him. He knew how lucky he was, at eighteen, to have landed a job on the *Kansas City Star*. The *Star* was one of the most widely respected newspapers in the United States, and the opportunity to train in its newsroom was the goal of many young men who wished to become reporters.

Ernest arrived in Missouri in mid-October, and was met at the Kansas City train station by his Uncle Tyler. At first he was happy to see his uncle, to be close to family in a city full of strangers. But even the train trip from Oak Park had added to Ernest's sense of his own maturity—he had crossed the Mississippi River!—and Tyler Hemingway's house began in just a few days to seem confining. Uncle Tyler reminded Ernest of his father—pious, formal, a believer in propriety and discipline. As though to annoy Uncle Tyler and his wife, Ernest quickly adopted a rough appearance and manner, upset a neighborhood girl on their first (and only) date, and began to look for another place to live.

Fortunately he had an option. Carl Edgar, a young businessman, was a friend Ernest had met in northern Michigan. They'd fished and hunted together, and got along well although Edgar was older than Ernest. Ernest made arrangements to share an apartment with his friend. In addition to moving in, Ernest wasted no time in giving his roommate the nickname "Odgar." They did not see much of each other—Ernest was at the *Star* early, and business responsibilities often kept Carl Edgar at his desk late into the night.

Although always willing to talk a night away with his roommate, Ernest had little time for socializing. The *Star* was working him too hard; he was in the newsroom constantly. It was an environment Ernest took to immediately, relishing the long hours, the constant attention to detail, the insistence upon accuracy and clarity. The *Kansas City Star* imposed a thirty-day probationary period on all new reporters, and Ernest was determined to pass through it successfully. As far as he was concerned, he would be happy to live at the *Star*. He was earning sixty dollars a month.

As with all cub reporters, Ernest spent much of his time writing obituaries, capsule reports, and other one- or two-paragraph articles that were inserted to fill space or give balance and variety to a page. Subject matter and size did not matter to Ernest—he took his time with each piece, working over the sentences and structure. If he was assigned to write two paragraphs he wanted them to be as good as anything else in the *Star*.

His diligence and dedication brought him to the attention of the *Star*'s editorial staff. Because they took pride in the *Star*'s distinctive voice and tone, the editors enjoyed training young reporters in the paper's style, rather than retraining more seasoned journalists who had apprenticed elsewhere. Much of the training was done by C. G. ("Pete") Wellington, the paper's assistant city editor, and much of Wellington's training was based upon the *Kansas City Star* style sheet for reporters and writers.

The style sheet was Ernest's textbook as a cub reporter. There were 110 rules contained in the style sheet, and Wellington and the other editors insisted that cub reporters study them until they knew them as well, and as unconsciously, as they knew how to breathe.

Ernest did study the style sheet, going through it again and again, not simply memorizing the rules, but concentrating on them until he understood and could put into practice their meaning. The rules seized his attention, and he never forgot them, using them as a code as important as those of fishing or boxing. He could recite them in his sleep.

Use short sentences . . . avoid adjectives and adverbs . . . use verbs that are strong and make the story come alive . . . be positive . . . make sure all slang is fresh and new. All the rules seemed sound and valuable to Ernest. He put them to work, and worked with them and on them, from his first day on the job. They were strong rules, but they were also flexible, permitting their master to achieve a great variety of effects within the stylistic framework of the newspaper. Ernest wanted to become their master. He saw that simplicity and brevity—the use of just a few words—could achieve much that was impossible for the formal, complex, and rhetorical Victorian prose that had for so long dominated journalism and literature.

At the end of thirty days, Ernest was rewarded with an assignment. He had passed the probationary period and would now be serving as a reporter. It was another mark of his manhood, another symbol of his growth. He enjoyed the success, and took great pride on those occasions when Pete Wellington would throw an arm around his shoulder and talk colleague-to-colleague.

Ernest's assignments gave him exactly what he wanted. He covered government buildings for a while, but soon was allowed to search for stories in more exciting surroundings. He would travel from the Fifteenth Street police station to Union Station to Kansas City General Hospital, eyes open, notebook out, in search of news.

At the police station Ernest wrote stories of small crimes and hoped for something juicier. Union Station offered the prospects of large crowds moving, an occasional celebrity, and the variety of drifters, pickpockets, and con men who preyed upon travelers. Kansas City General Hospital gave Ernest a wealth of material, from accident victims to violent crimes. An ambulance being assigned automatically captured Ernest's attention— where was it going? Who had been hurt, and how? As often as not, Ernest talked his way into the ambulance, a grin on his face as he rode beneath the flashing lights and siren.

Ernest understood the rules of the style sheet, and followed them, but he was less attentive to the personnel rules by which he was supposed to abide. He would leap into an ambulance without calling the city desk to inform them of his whereabouts. More than once, he missed a story because he had ridden off in the first ambulance assigned, only to find that it was traveling to treat a minor, and not newsworthy, injury. Ernest was warned about his misplaced enthusiasm, but his habits would not change. He felt that he had to be present at any possibility of action, and the sound of a siren was to Ernest a call to arms.

On the whole, though, he got on well at the paper, and Wellington, among others, thought that Ernest Hemingway might be a by-line to watch. The boy's command of the language seemed to grow with each story filed, and his almost instinctive control of a story's structure seemed a real gift. Certainly it was a gift for anyone as young as Ernest. Although the *Star* insisted upon the classic Ws of newspaper writing—who, what, when, where, why—there was a great deal of leniency allowed in their presentation. Use of dialogue was encouraged. The organization of the story was left to the reporter's discretion and ability, as long as he achieved clarity and drama. Stories, and the people in them, should be made to come as alive as they would in a piece of fiction.

Ernest quickly began to earn praise not only from his editors but also from the other reporters in the city room. He frequently got a congratulatory clap on the back or the offer of a drink from an older reporter. The older reporter to whom Ernest most constantly gravitated was Lionel Calhoun Moise, a veteran of many years in many different city rooms, one of the few reporters on the *Star* who had not been trained there since apprenticeship.

Moise enjoyed talking about reporting, and Ernest listened raptly to every word. There should be no difference, Moise argued, between the stylistic and grammatical requirements of fine reporting and fine literature. Each sought purity of language, dramatic presentation, and sense of story. Moise had little use for experimental fiction, although he was well versed in modern literature. Ernest was somewhat in awe of Moise's skills as a reporter, and even more impressed by the man's ability to control a room with his personality and to tell long tales of drinking and brawling while still turning in a day's work.

There were others in the office with whom Ernest grew friendly, and all of them were eager to share their ambitions. When Ernest received a food package from Oak Park, he often brought it to the office and shared it with the others as they talked. It seemed that everyone on the paper planned eventually to write a novel. Ernest bragged that his novel would be a great novel, and would make his name. Moise advised each of them that the only way to learn to write was to write . . . and write and *write*. But it was still fun to talk, to share a piece of cake or a drink with fellow reporters and listen as they spun their dreams.

Ernest still dreamed of seeing action in Europe, and during the winter he tried repeatedly to enlist. Each time he was turned down because of his eyesight. The war was much on his mind as he covered wire service stories of its progress or noted the number of tanks being shipped out. He could not tolerate the thought that he might miss altogether his chance to see combat.

Throughout early 1918 Ernest tried to get into the service, and at the same time he showed even more improvement as a reporter. He took in every detail of a story, and then wrote it so that it came to life on the page. He made his rounds in search of news, indulging his fascination with gamblers, criminals, people on the lowest end of the social spectrum. He even wrote a story about a young prostitute. The piece was very good, and people went out of their way at the *Star* to tell him so.

Ernest enjoyed playing veteran reporter to new cubs, though he was often younger than they. One cub to whom he introduced himself was Ted Brumback, a wealthy young man who'd lost an eye in a college golfing accident. More impressive than the missing eye to Ernest was the fact that Brumback, despite his disability, had served in Europe as an ambulance driver for the American Field Service. Obviously there was a way around the medical refusals Ernest had faced.

In April 1918, Ernest and "Brummy" (Ernest still assigned nicknames immediately) were covering the news wire when a story came in describing the Red Cross's need for volunteers to serve in Italy. Ernest and Ted had their applications out before they even began to rewrite the story. By the end of April they had turned in their resignations and were awaiting orders from Red Cross headquarters.

Ernest left the *Kansas City Star* less than seven months after joining it. It had been quite an experience—the equivalent, he was sure, of years of college journalism courses. In college he would have received grades; at the *Star* he saw his words in print. He said goodbye to Pete Wellington, Lionel Moise, and the others he'd learned so much from. Then he, Ted Brumback, and Carl Edgar set off for a brief expedition to Walloon Lake.

It was even briefer than they had planned. Orders arrived

insisting that Ernest and Ted be in New York City by May 8, 1918. He returned to Oak Park, bid a hectic farewell to his parents, accepted $150 from his father, and boarded the train for New York.

Orientation in New York City was no less of a whirlwind. When his uniform was issued, Ernest did not find it glamorous enough and rushed out to buy an expensive pair of boots to lend more dash to his appearance. He was proud of his honorary second lieutenant's bars, and could not remember standing straighter in his life than when he marched as a platoon guide in a Fifth Avenue parade for President Woodrow Wilson.

There was hardly any time to see New York. Inoculations, regulations, and training kept Ernest busy until May 21 when he boarded the *Chicago* for his voyage to Europe. They sailed with the morning tide on May 23, 1918.

Ernest stood at the rail and watched the harbor recede. He was leaving America. He had traveled by boat before, on a steamboat along the length of Lake Michigan to Walloon Lake. But this was the Atlantic Ocean and his destination was Italy. Everything was strange, exciting, new. Everything appealed to the skills he had acquired at the *Star*. Ernest took it all in, sights and smells carefully and completely stored for future use. He was a writer going to his first war.

FIVE

WAR

DURING THE CROSSING, Ernest spent hours at the rail, squinting at the horizon. The Red Cross physicians who had examined him prescribed glasses to correct his vision, but Ernest would not wear them, not even to help him spot the enemy ships he searched for. There were no enemy ships, nothing at all to see, and Ernest complained to Ted Brumback of the dullness of the voyage. Brumback, who had been to the war once already, said nothing.

The *Chicago* landed in Bordeaux shortly before the end of May. Ernest took time to sample French cooking and—more important, he thought—French wine before boarding a train for Paris. He and Brumback arrived in Paris as the city was under fire by "Big Bertha," the German artillery piece that lobbed shells dozens of miles. Ernest's nose for news was as keen as his sense of excitement, and he hired a taxi to follow the explosions. He hoped the gun was firing in a pattern so that his chase would lead him and Brumback to the opportunity of witnessing a shell's impact. But Bertha's pattern that day was random, and although they saw a few fresh craters, Ernest and Ted Brumback could not close in on an actual landing. They finally gave up and were returning to their quarters when one of Bertha's projectiles passed whistling overhead and struck the hotel where they were staying. The building was not badly damaged, and Ernest was thrilled to have seen his first action. Now, although he resolved to return to Paris, he was eager to move on to Italy.

He shipped out within a few days, bound with other volunteers for Milan. The scenery en route was as wonderful as anything Ernest had ever encountered or even imagined. He gaped at the splendor of the Alps, made notes of every trout stream he passed over, delighted in the long Mount Cenis tunnel. Milan lay ahead and Ernest wondered how long it would be before he was more than a simple witness to action.

He received his answer immediately. On his first day in Milan an explosion destroyed a munitions factory, killing dozens and wounding many more. Ernest joined in the rescue operation, searching for survivors, carrying out the dead. This was no lark, as had been the mad chase for Big Bertha's damage. This was destruction on a large scale, and Ernest saw things he had never seen before. When the wounded were removed, Ernest and his companions were assigned to gather pieces of bodies from fences and trees around the factory. Ernest had never seen anything like it, but he could not stop looking, could not stop taking in every detail of the appearances of the dead. He noticed the expressions on their faces, how bodies did not blow apart along anatomical lines. He would never forget the dead women, some of them hairless, many of them with their insides torn out as a result of explosive concussion. What in Oak Park had prepared him for this? War would be as much of an education as anything else on earth.

Within two days Ernest was assigned to American Red Cross Section Four, along with Ted Brumback and others he had met on the voyage over. They were to be posted at Schio, a small town twenty-four miles from Milan. Schio lay in hilly country at the foot of the mountains, and Ernest's job was to drive an ambulance up winding roads over steep drops, and then return over the same treacherous territory bearing wounded. At night a blackout was imposed and the route became even more dangerous.

Ernest worked twenty-four hours on duty and twenty-four hours off. When he was on his own time he continued to develop his taste for wine, boasting of the quantities he could drink. He wrote home irregularly, letters containing manly references to the likeliness of death and bragging statements detailing the numbers of enemy helmets and weapons he had captured. The letters could not completely mask his homesickness, and once he asked for friends to write him, to remind him of what home was like.

He also found time to contribute a brief piece to Section Four's newspaper, *Ciao*, writing in the Ring Lardner manner he had affected in high school. There was not a great deal of time for writing; there were too many new friends to meet, too many distractions. Italy offered more than the romance of war, he found, and Ernest often simply watched the people on the street. The women were occasionally flirtatious, and Ernest was taken with the way Italian men followed them around openly. Some of the volunteers visited bordellos; all of them heard Ernest's boasts about an amorous high school life. His smile was wide and bright, and he was always eager to introduce himself to fellow Americans. Some of them wanted to be writers themselves. One young volunteer, John Dos Passos, hit it off well with Ernest, though they spoke only briefly.

It soon became clear that the roads were the greatest dangers near Schio. Ernest set about finding an assignment that promised real action. When some members of Section Four were given the opportunity to drive into a battle zone, Ernest immediately volunteered. He was turned down, and he grew livid. How could he be left out of such an adventure? He searched harder for a more dramatic posting, threatening to leave the Ambulance Corps if he did not find one.

In late June he volunteered to man a canteen close to the front. The Red Cross canteens were spots at which combat soldiers rested, wrote letters, listened to music, and received chocolate and cigarettes. Best of all, thought Ernest, the canteens were close to the lines of battle.

He was assigned to establish a canteen near Fossalta on the

Piave River. At first there was little to do—supplies were in short supply and arrived slowly. Ernest quickly grew restless, taking what comfort he could in the battle sounds that, in Fossalta, he could hear clearly. When his provisions did begin to come in, Ernest applied all of his energy to the establishment of the canteen. It was an important service, boosting the soldiers' morale, and often in the evenings Ernest loaded himself with cigarettes, candy, and postcards, and pedaled his bicycle to the trenches to distribute them in person. The soldiers were always happy to see Ernest, who seemed a typical American boy, good-looking and happy. They called him, in reference to both his honorary commission and his poor Italian, *tenente.*

On the evening of July 8, 1918, Ernest bicycled to the forward trenches, carrying chocolate and cigarettes. He made his way slowly through the dark night. It was very hot, with artillery and mortar fire being exchanged by both sides. Flares occasionally exploded overhead, turning the night into day. Ernest went from soldier to soldier, speaking briefly with them, offering them a smoke or a candy bar.

Midnight passed. A shell shrieked over, closer than any before. When it exploded it scattered shrapnel in all directions, flying fragments of hot metal that could shred a human being. The explosion seized Ernest and flung him as though he were weightless, and then the shrapnel cut into his legs. He was in too much pain even to pass out, and all the sounds around him mingled into a single roar. Gradually he fought for control and began sorting things out. His legs felt as though they were bathed in hot water. He was lying next to a dead man, but a soldier nearby was wailing in agony. Ernest crawled to the wounded soldier and grasped him firmly. He did not know if he could walk, but he gathered all of his strength, lifted the soldier across his shoulders, rose slowly, and turned toward the back of the lines where he could get medical attention. He had to get there first and could move only hesitantly, balancing the soldier, struggling to control his own legs. His fine boots felt as though they were made of rubber.

The command post was 150 yards away, and Ernest had traveled barely a third of the distance when an Austrian machine gun bullet hit him in the right knee and he went down. Yet, incredibly, with mangled legs and a heavy burden, he covered the final hundred yards. Neither he nor any of the Italians ever understood how. But he did, and did not allow himself to pass out until the Italian soldier was borne away for treatment. Then Ernest drifted in and out of consciousness, overhearing the doctors agree that such terrible chest wounds could not be survived. Ernest roused himself enough to demand the removal of his tunic—he had no chest wounds. What the doctors saw was blood from the soldier Ernest had carried. He was nearly delirious and told the doctors that he could not allow the Austrians to capture his goats. Then he passed out again.

The medical station had been destroyed by the shelling, and Ernest was carried to a crumbling, roofless stable to await evacuation by ambulance. The Ambulance Corps was overloaded, however, and Ernest lay in the stable for two hours, surrounded by dead men and men who were dying. More than once Ernest thought he was dying himself, and it was the strangest feeling he had ever experienced. All around him men moaned, artillery pieces fired, more shells exploded. The warm water on Ernest's legs had been replaced by what felt like hot nails driven by devils. He thought that the ambulance would never come, and that death might be preferable to the agony in his legs. But when the ambulance did arrive Ernest insisted that it first take the wounded soldiers, and come back for him after the fighting men were removed.

Finally his stretcher was loaded into an ambulance and he was driven to a medical station, where he was treated by doctors who knew him. They immediately injected him with morphine and anti-tetanus, and then set to work on his legs. At the station that night the surgeons removed twenty-eight shell fragments, but there were nearly two hundred more too deeply embedded to be removed under battlefield conditions. The doctors took care to bandage their tenente's legs carefully and wish him well before he was carried to a field hospital.

It was July 15, less than a week before his nineteenth birthday, when Ernest was sent to Milan to receive proper medical attention. The field doctors had done a good job and there was no infection. At the Ospedale Croce Rossa Americana (American Red Cross Hospital) in Milan, Ernest's wounds began to be tabulated. It was an amazing count: his legs had received 227 pieces of metal from the mortar shell, and he had taken machine gun bullets in the right knee and foot. That he survived seemed a miracle; that he had carried a soldier 150 yards was the stuff of legend.

Ernest enjoyed the celebrity that accompanied his heroism. Newspapers in Italy and the United States carried stories about his actions, for he was the first American to be wounded in Italy. Ernest's letters home were full of patter dismissive of his heroics—they were just what he did under the circumstances. He was more interested in describing the nature of his wounds and, with some precision, the nature of the treatment and operations undertaken by his doctors. He was adamant in his insistence that they not amputate his leg. Ernest had told his surgeons of his father's skills, and they were solicitous of Ernest's opinion: would Dr. Clarence Hemingway approve of their surgery?

He also enjoyed talking with the nurses in the Ospedale, and one of them soon became the focus of his attention and charm. Her name was Agnes Hannah von Kurowsky, a tall young woman from Pennsylvania who was seven years older than Ernest. She had worked in a library before becoming a nurse, and had arrived in Italy in June, as had Ernest. She visited Ernest frequently, enjoying their conversations, perhaps a bit put off by his bluster, laughing as he assigned nicknames to the other nurses on the ward. As though his wounds were not evidence enough, Ernest sought to prove his courage, and would take a big drink of brandy as an anesthetic and then use a penknife to dig metal fragments from his legs. Other times he whistled, as his father had taught him, to show that the pain did not bother him.

Agnes distracted him as well. He was in love with her, and occasionally she would allow him to kiss her. Ernest lay in the hospital bed for more than a month, bravely facing operations, accepting congratulations on his nineteenth birthday. Soon he was accepting greater congratulations: there was talk that he would receive a medal. Ernest shrugged the possibility off when others mentioned it, but sometimes he mentioned it himself. He kept a bottle of brandy in his room at all times, and would share it with his fellow wounded, comparing the nature of their wounds with his own.

He wanted Agnes all for himself, and as September neared he told her he wanted to marry her. Although, indulging his fondness for nicknames, she allowed Ernest to call himself "Kid" and referred to herself as "Mrs. Kid," Agnes refused to accept his proposal. Nor would she sleep with him, despite the increasing fervor of Ernest's feelings and the intensity with which he communicated his desire. The relationship with Ernest was more than a flirtation for Agnes—she cared deeply for him—but it was less than an affair.

Throughout the end of the summer, Ernest's legs continued to heal. He had stitches and scars and would catalogue them for anyone who would listen. The bandages began to come off, although his right leg remained in a splint to allow the knee to mend. He was allowed into a wheelchair, and in the fall Marcelline saw Ernest in a newsreel. She and her parents hurried to a nearby town where the newsreel would play next, and sat in the theater crying happily over the sight of Ernest in Italy.

Soon he was able to walk with a cane, and took care to dress himself carefully for his appearances in Milan. He thought he looked quite dashing, and the nurses agreed, taking pictures of him to send home to Oak Park. In September Ernest's heroism was acknowledged by promotion to the rank of first lieutenant, which allowed him to serve in the regular Italian army. He began to speak of action again, and wondered how long it would be until he was sufficiently healthy to return to the front.

Ernest continued to pay court to Agnes, accompanying her to horse races, proud to stand next to such a striking young woman, and equally proud of the wound stripes and insignia sewn onto his uniform. The Italians welcomed Ernest warmly, and when they learned how he had received his wounds they treated him almost like family: people bought him drinks and meals, happy to serve the hero.

Despite his pain, which sometimes drove him to constant whistling, Ernest found something of a holiday atmosphere in the warm fall in Milan. How could he not? He was young; he had proved himself in battle; he was in love. But the war went on outside Milan, and early in October Agnes volunteered to go to Florence. There was an epidemic there and nurses were badly needed. Ernest was devastated but was unable to stop her. She departed soon after telling him, and until she did Ernest followed her around like a wounded pet. Didn't she understand what she meant to him? Didn't she know how much he loved her and wanted her?

Without Agnes, Ernest fell into a depression. He wrote her constantly, sometimes several letters a day, and when he was not writing her he was drinking. He began to smoke cigarettes and to cultivate an attitude of world-weariness. Not long after Agnes left for Florence, he wrote his family and spoke of how easy it was to die. He thought that he understood death, that it was just about the simplest thing in the world to understand. Continuing to live, he wrote, was what was hard.

Agnes wrote letters to Ernest as well, and while they were not so frequent as his they were filled with emotion and endearments. Ernest carried the letters with him and read them as he drank. He spoke expertly of love, sex, and war with his friends, and as October came to a close he decided to return to the front. He went to Schio, and from there on to Mount Grappa, where a large battle was shaping up. He watched an all-night artillery duel much larger than the one in which he'd been wounded, and he knew that there would be many men in need of evacuation. By morning, though, it was Ernest who had to be evacuated: he had come down with jaundice and was returned to a hospital bed in Milan.

He would not linger there long. Within a week he was up and getting slowly about. He went for a drink on November 3, 1918, and learned that Italy and America had ceased hostilities. It was time for celebration and Ernest, always at ease with strangers, introduced himself to a British officer sitting nearby. This officer was Major Eric Dorman-Smith, twenty-three and in the infantry. He shared his combat experiences with Ernest. Ernest told Dorman-Smith of his own experiences, transmuting his volunteer heroism into a story of battle at close quarters with experienced enemy troops. Dorman-Smith and Ernest grew close in the course of the day, and soon were spending their free time together. Ernest dubbed his new friend "Chink" and in turn was known simply as "Hem."

Agnes came back to Milan shortly afterward, but the visit was brief. They resumed their affection, although Agnes told Ernest that he needed to give some thought to his future. He was considering staying in Italy for a while, enjoying the good life, trading on his heroism. He could get a year's leave at full pay as a result of his action. Agnes offered advice that sounded as though it came from Oak Park: he must find something constructive to do; he must take advantage of his gifts and use them to make a contribution. Then, too quickly, she was off to another epidemic-ridden hospital.

Shortly before Christmas Ernest appeared at the hospital. He was dressed impeccably, boots polished, medals gleaming, wound insignia bright. He leaned on a cane and spoke of the action he had seen. The soldiers in the hospital, wounded, sick, and unshaven, laughed at him. He had written his parents once that there were no heroes, but with Agnes, and with Chink Dorman-Smith, all he wanted to speak of was heroism, courage, death in battle. It was a pose, Agnes told him, and one that offended people. She told him to put the war behind him and to go home to his family.

Christmas neared. It was Ernest's first holiday season away from the United States. He could remember the wonderful smells with which Dr. Hemingway's Christmas treats filled the house. He had a brother, now nearly four years old. His leg was better and he was able to get around easily. He continued to hope that Agnes would marry him and did not cease to write her every day. Ernest and Eric Dorman-Smith made the rounds of parties in Milan, but Agnes remained at the hospital.

Despite the attractions of Italy, and the offer of a year on full salary without duties, Ernest came to see Agnes's point. He could return to Europe later, but now he should go home. He wanted to see his family and friends. He was eager to begin turning his experiences into stories, excited about starting to write seriously once more. He arranged for passage home in early January. Then, as though desperate to take in as much as he could before departure, he left Milan for a tour of southern Italy. He wanted to see Sicily but boasted to Chink that he could not because his hostess was too passionate and kept him confined to bed. He and Agnes exchanged a few last letters in Europe, and soon it was time to board the S.S. *Giuseppe Verdi* for the voyage home.

SIX

VETERAN

ERNEST ARRIVED IN NEW YORK on January 21, 1919, and the event was detailed in the *New York Sun* the next morning. Just as Ernest, working for the *Star,* had kept his eyes open for celebrities passing through the train station, the *Sun's* reporter waited on the dock for Ernest's appearance. According to the article, Ernest was not only the first American wounded in Italy, but he had received more wounds than any other soldier or civilian in Europe. Despite his wounds, the article implied, Ernest returned to bitter combat for several weeks before the war ended. At the *Star* Ernest had learned to check and verify facts, but now he did not challenge the *Sun's* reporter or the story as printed. He joined friends for an all-night celebration in New York before catching the train to Chicago.

Dr. Hemingway had wept when Ernest left for war, and his cheeks shone with tears on his son's return. His sisters and brother were at the house to greet him. Grace seemed unchanged. Most important, as he stepped into his home he saw two letters from Agnes in Italy. Using his cane, Ernest went slowly up to his bedroom to read the letters. Agnes was working hard, and had met President Wilson on his tour of Europe. She said that she missed Ernest; he missed her more than he could say.

Oak Park seemed quieter than a hospital, and it certainly possessed none of the distractions he had grown accustomed to

71

in Italy. He brought some brandy home with him, but had to keep it more closely hidden from his parents than he ever had from the ward nurses in the Ospedale. Everything was quiet; everything seemed drab and ordinary.

He took to lingering in his room until noon, spending the still mornings reading, exercising his toes, dreaming of Italy and Agnes. He had little to say to his family. Although he showed some interest in medical books and the AMA *Journal,* Ernest had no intention of rekindling his parents' ambitions: he was simply curious about his wounds and how they would affect him.

Brandy was not the only thing he'd brought home from Italy. With him had come a large trunk filled with war souvenirs, each of which had, or for which Ernest invented, a dramatic story. Two eleven-year-old neighborhood girls developed a crush on the romantic young veteran, and Ernest fired a star shell for them, the flare lighting Oak Park as others had lighted the Piave battlefield. Dr. Hemingway especially enjoyed seeing the star shells fired.

When the flares died out Ernest was still in Oak Park, and he tried to communicate to his family the different world he'd discovered overseas. He insisted that Marcelline sample the brandy, telling her from experience of the great pleasures and comforts alcohol offered. There was nothing wrong with drinking, he said, or with smoking cigarettes, or with any of the other things Oak Park propriety preached against so loudly. It was all part of life, and life was meant to be sampled, indulged, tested, and explored. In Oak Park, Ernest said, everyone was only half alive.

He did not feel fully alive any more. Agnes's letters continued to arrive, but increasingly contained references to other wounded young men. Ernest wondered if he were being replaced in her affections. Books could distract him only some of the time, for he realized that no matter how good a book, its experiences came to the reader secondhand. So many books were only imitations of life. He did not feel ready to begin writing once more, but he felt that when he did he would have to use his own experiences carefully. He did not want them, still so vivid, to seem secondhand.

The Italian community in Chicago provided amusement when Ernest went there for delicacies he'd grown to love during the war. A group of Italians, some of them opera singers, decided to throw a party for the hero, and nearly fifty of them arrived at the Hemingway home one Sunday. They brought large amounts of Italian food and wine, and were much taken with Grace's elaborate music room. The neighborhood grew resonant with passionate arias and speeches acclaiming the courage of *Tenente* Hemingway. Despite Dr. and Mrs. Hemingway's objections, wine flowed freely and the party lasted all afternoon. The next Sunday the Italians returned, with friends, for a larger, louder, and more drunken party. Enough was enough, Dr. Hemingway said, and from then on Ernest had to visit his friends in Chicago.

The local newspaper printed an interview with Ernest in which he was modest and almost bashful about his exploits. He gave a speech at his old high school that was livelier, its highlight being Ernest's display of the bloody and shredded trousers he'd been wearing when wounded.

As spring neared he received from Agnes a letter that confirmed his fears: she had fallen in love with an officer in the Italian army. She wrote to wish him well, and to explain that he would always have a special place in her affections. The news drove Ernest to bed with a fever, and when he rose it was with a bitter determination not only to get over Agnes but also to condemn her in every way possible. He wrote to her fellow nurses, telling of his hopes that she would be in an accident and disfigured. He claimed that she meant nothing to him, and that he had cured his heartbreak with an alcoholic binge and more than a few young women. He did not need Agnes Hannah von Kurowsky, he contended, and he hoped she would be very happy with whatever disasters life brought to her.

His parents began dropping reminders that it was time to begin making plans. They wanted him to attend college in the fall, and were curious as to his course of study. Ernest spent more time in his bedroom, thinking, brooding, reading. It was not long before he turned to the typewriter and started putting down words that he hoped would reflect all he had learned in the past year. One of his stories dealt with a battle against the Austrians along the Piave River. Ernest worked to get the details correct—he remembered everything he had seen—but the story lacked the immediacy he hoped to achieve. He worked harder at the typewriter.

As the weather warmed, Oak Park became too confining. In Italy he had dreamed of the trout streams of northern Michigan. Now he could go there, and he planned the first expedition of the summer, leaving his parents' home shortly after the end of May. He was not yet ready for the deep woods and spent June at Horton Bay, where he worked to get his legs in shape for the long hikes that lay ahead. Even Horton Bay was too civilized, too proper. By July he would be ready to get away from everything.

He traveled in company with a friend, Bill Smith, pushing deep into wild country. The trip lasted a week, and for days they saw no houses or any signs of people. They came upon bear and deer. They talked or did not talk as their moods struck them. Better than anything were the trout, and they fished rivers that had seen few—if any—fishermen before. Ernest relaxed into the rhythms and timings of the fly rod, flicking the line gracefully up, back, and out, presenting his fly or worm on the end of a silk leader, coming alive as his rod did, bending to the fury of the fish. He caught as many as thirty trout a day, and the rivers he fished became part of him forever.

When the trek was over he returned to Walloon Lake, where the family had gathered for the summer as always. It was hard to sleep in a bed after sleeping in the wilderness. Even a tent near Windemere was not the same. It was too civilized; it had too many rules. Grace continued to press Ernest for his plans, lecturing him to accept the beauty of life and outgrow the hostility he displayed to virtually everyone.

Although he felt fully alive only in the woods, Ernest was obliged to stay close to Windemere for the time being. He had returned from his camping trip determined to make his name as a writer, and that meant that he would have to submit his stories to magazines. Edwin Balmer, who was a professional writer, lived across from Windemere, and Ernest sought his advice. Balmer explained to Ernest the mechanics of manuscript preparation, story submission, and literary professionalism. Ernest listened intently, intending to learn the rules of fiction writing as fully as he had the rules of newspaper reporting. Balmer provided a list of magazines and their editors, and Ernest began to plan a vigorous campaign of submissions.

By August he had had enough of Windemere, his parents, and what seemed to him only half-life—or half-death. The only cure would be trout fishing under starry skies. With Bill Smith and two other friends, Ernest traveled by car to the edge of the wilderness, feeling more alive, at least more aware, each mile. Again, there was magic in the wilderness. Trout, cigarettes, whiskey, and companionship were the elements of the spell, and the spirits of the four fishermen could not be dampened even by the beginning of their return trip. They laughed and sang in the car, and as they passed through a small town took turns shooting out the streetlamps with Ernest's rifle. It was like still being in the woods, where they made their own rules. The police officer who stopped the car moments later felt differently, and although he did not arrest or cite the young men, his presence made it clear that they had returned to a world where behavior had to be tempered with judgment and morality, or at least common sense.

That world might have its hold on Bill Smith and the others—they returned to Illinois for work or school—but Ernest set out on another fishing trip almost immediately. He found two more friends and made of them a "gang," as he called his groups. It was as convivial as the others, with Ernest assuming leadership. He knew the woods, and showed his friends the ins and outs of camping. He was an expert campfire cook. He caught more trout than his companions, and he could drink more liquor. Around the fire in the evenings he held forth on war and death, and when the conversation turned to women Ernest spoke profoundly from his largely imaginary experiences.

His legs were strong now, and he worked to eliminate his limp. He did not wish to be thought of as a cripple. On his camping trips he was worrying at a decision, and late in the summer he made up his mind. He would not stay in Oak Park during the coming winter. He would only visit it for a few days and then not until deep autumn. The Dilworths, of Horton Bay, owned a restaurant and cottage, and he could take a room there. He would be in Michigan during a new season. It would be a good place and time to do some serious writing. He went to stay with the Dilworths.

Summer dwindled, and Ernest helped with the local potato harvest. His stories grew longer, but were not yet ready to be published. Edwin Balmer had told him that the one thing a professional writer must have is discipline. Without it, without long hours at the typewriter on a regular schedule, no writer developed. Throughout September and October Ernest imposed on himself a fierce discipline. Every morning he rose and went to his desk and worked with words. He wanted to exercise his prose as he had exercised his body: to get it in shape, to make it ready.

He wrote of the war, for it was still much on his mind, but there were new experiences to write of as well. For all of his bragging, in conversations and in letters, about the experiences he'd had with women, it was not until that fall, a war veteran alone in civilian life for the first time, that Ernest had a physical affair. Soon after, he left Horton Bay, visited his parents for as brief a stay as possible, and settled into a rooming house in Petoskey, Michigan.

76

In Petoskey he wrote, paid some attention to local high school girls, and assembled a new gang for drinking and storytelling. He talked of his war experiences to a women's volunteer organization. The freedom and independence of his life were wonderful, but before winter was well begun it was clear that he would have to find work. He was invited by a wealthy family to come to Toronto and serve as companion to their crippled son. The boy, Ralph Connable, was nearly Ernest's age and the two got on well. Ralph's parents were impressed with Ernest and offered him the use of their house and servants while they wintered in Palm Beach. Ernest accepted the offer immediately, and arrived in Toronto early in January 1920.

The opportunities presented by the Connables' offer were ideal, and within a few days Mr. Connable had introduced Ernest to the features editors of the *Toronto Star*. Ernest studied the weekly paper, learned its requirements, and began submitting freelance articles, light and humorous pieces that caught on with the readership. By spring he'd received a raise in the rate he was paid. His short stories, however, were still being returned with rejection slips.

In his articles Ernest attempted to deal with World War I, but obliquely, drawing on observation rather than experience. Some of the pieces were sad, portraits of people pawning war medals for a few dollars; others were more bitter, heartfelt attacks on those who lacked the courage to go to war and out of fear dodged the draft. He could also be quite funny, as in a piece about student barbers. He was attempting to stretch his range, writing about a variety of subjects, testing his abilities with different backgrounds, circumstances, and tones.

The Connables took pride in Ernest's accomplishments, and Ernest was pleased to be treated as a peer rather than as a child. He was an adult now, moving socially in company with adults. He wrote out a detailed sheet of gambling instructions, complete with diagrams and formulas, for the Connables' trip to Palm Beach. According to Ernest, his knowledge of gambling had been acquired through close study during a wild youth.

By the summer of 1920 he was ready to leave Toronto. He could continue to write freelance features, submitting them by mail. Ernest returned to Walloon Lake with Bill Smith, and set about planning a season's expeditions. He was also thinking about the fall, planning to ship out for the Orient with Ted Brumback.

It was harder than ever for Ernest to be with his family. His mother, now forty-eight, lectured him constantly, insisting that he was not doing his share of the chores. Dr. Hemingway felt called upon to write an admonitory letter in which he expressed deep disappointment with Ernest. Ernest was rude and offensive in behavior and language; it was time for him to grow up and begin to act like an adult. Grace was not having an easy emotional time that summer, and Ernest's childishness was only making her life more difficult.

Ernest would not be repressed, and he certainly could not take being told that he was not an adult. He had done too much and seen too much, and it was up to his parents to understand that he set his own ways and kept his own hours. Late in the summer he and Ted Brumback took several girls, including Ursula and Sunny Hemingway, on a midnight picnic at a beach on Walloon Lake. They did not return until after three in the morning, and found Grace Hemingway waiting up for them. The girls were grounded for the rest of the season. And Ernest was told to leave the Hemingway property.

Grace tried to explain, one last time, her disappointment with Ernest, and sent him a long letter full of platitudes. He must remember his obligation to Jesus Christ, he must find in God the guidance he so desperately needed, he must overcome his selfishness and sloth, he must abandon all of his bad habits and undertake to develop a code of sound Christian ethics and moral sense. Until he did these things, his mother wrote, she would have no love left for him.

Ernest read the letter, announced that he no longer had a home, and then left for a week of trout fishing in the deep woods. He visited his family occasionally, and endeavored to remain civil in the presence of his parents. His father sided with Grace, and was cool and distant toward Ernest. It was clear that part of Ernest's life was over. He helped with the harvest, then moved to northern Chicago to live with Y. K. Smith, Bill's brother. Ernest was twenty-one now, a man by the calendar as well as by experience and attitude, and it was time for him to be away from home, whether his family would have him or not. He would do all right in Chicago.

SEVEN

HADLEY

CHICAGO OFFERED RHYTHM and excitement. Hemingway was living with a good gang, more than a few of whom were writers trying to establish themselves. They had much to talk about, and the parties they threw were loud and boisterous, with Hemingway contributing more than his share of the noise and energy. He flirted madly with many girls, but it was not until October 1921 that a young woman seriously attracted him.

Her name was Hadley Richardson. She was from St. Louis, she was tall, she had red hair, her eyes were bright with both life and pain, and she was twenty-eight years old. Ernest Hemingway was taken with her from the first moment he saw her, and he did not need long to learn of her background.

Hadley's father had killed himself when she was twelve years old. Since then she'd lived with her mother. In her early teens she had attended a private school, where she met Bill Smith's sister Katy. After graduation Hadley attended Bryn Mawr, but withdrew to return to her mother, whose apron strings were long and restrictive. Mrs. Richardson charted Hadley's course in life, telling her what to study, what to wear, what to do, and who to see. The only serious beau in Hadley's life had been a forty-year-old friend of her mother's. Mrs. Richardson was determined that Hadley do as she said, insisting even on Hadley's attendance at séances and Ouija board readings.

In October 1920, Hadley arrived in Chicago for a visit with Katy Smith. Hadley was exhausted from a summer spent nursing her mother through the final stages of cancer. The years of domination were over, but Hadley was not yet free from her mother. She was shy and soft-spoken, self-effacing and without a great deal of confidence. She was not sure how to join in the gaiety of the parties she attended with Bill, Y.K., and Katy—not even certain she *could* join in.

Hemingway was wearing his uniform when they met, and its clean lines, polished leather, and bright insignia and medals made for quite a presence, even in the crowded room. Hadley could not help but notice the effect Hemingway had on the other men present. They crowded around him, and it seemed as though they glanced at him for approval. It was clear that he was their leader, unfailingly offering advice and expertise on drinking, love, and war. He moved constantly, dropping into a boxer's crouch for a second, standing perfectly erect to deliver a sermon, demonstrating the close combat techniques of Italian soldiers, staring hard while showing off the widest smile she'd ever seen. Sometimes it looked as though that smile would split his cheeks. He was at his best when devising nicknames, and he was delighted to learn that she already had a good one. From that moment he called her "Hash."

After three sparkling weeks Hadley returned to St. Louis. Hemingway's enthusiasm was contagious, and she was very susceptible. The quiet, withdrawn world her mother had created for her retreated a bit each time Hemingway laughed, and she wanted to see more of his world. They stayed in touch by mail.

Hemingway had plenty of time to write. He was trying to establish himself as a writer, but the market for his pieces had shrunk. Even his feature articles were selling infrequently. He had begun visiting his family at Oak Park for Sunday dinner each week. The food was wonderful, there was plenty of it, and the price was right. As a concession, he wrote his mother and hinted that he was taking her advice.

Near the end of 1920 Hemingway found a job as editorial assistant of the *Cooperative Commonwealth*, the monthly magazine of a direct mail venture that later collapsed into bankruptcy and scandal. In 1921, though, the magazine was thriving and for forty dollars a week Ernest Hemingway wrote copy, wrote advertisements, worked with typesetters, and helped lay out the pages for the printer. It was a job that called for a great deal of energy but it was not particularly challenging or demanding for Hemingway. He kept loose hours during the early weeks of the month, and long hours as deadlines neared. He managed to keep a full social schedule—loud, laughing talk over cheap wine and cigarettes—as well as working on stories and writing Hadley.

The letters to Hadley grew successively more serious. As with Agnes von Kurowsky, Hemingway was ready to profess his undying love before the object of that love was ready to receive it. Hadley's responses, both in Chicago and by mail, were carefully worded, affectionate but cautious. She was concerned about the differences in their ages and temperaments. She was certain that Hemingway had what was needed to become an important writer, but thought that he might derive more benefits than he knew from bachelor freedom. She did not want to be a burden to him.

Hemingway ignored her objections. He was strong and young. It was a time for adventure, not caution. He wanted Hadley to see that she was young and strong enough for anything. He was living on a budget and saving as much of his salary as he could. It was time to return to Europe—to life—and he wanted Hadley to come with him.

By March Hadley no longer denied that she was deeply in love with Hemingway. She had no relatives to tie her to the United States. In fact, with the death of her mother, Hadley received a trust fund of a few thousand dollars. The interest on it would help them survive overseas. Hemingway converted some of her earnings into Italian currency.

He was making literary as well as financial arrangements. Sherwood Anderson, a successful and influential writer, lived

nearby and Hemingway sought his advice on many things. All of
the writers in northern Chicago gathered around Anderson; his
apartment was something of a salon where ambitious young men
talked of the books they would write. Anderson was older, in his
mid-forties, and had already written an important book, *Winesburg, Ohio.* Published in 1919, the book had created something
of a scandal because of its sexual and emotional frankness. But
that frankness had also been praised by some critics, and there
was much admiration for Anderson's technique. *Winesburg,
Ohio* was not formally a novel, but a cycle of twenty brief stories
and one long one linked by geography and the observations of a
recurrent character. The stories looked at moments in the lives
of people living in and around a small Ohio town. Each of those
moments was perfectly captured, communicating to the reader
the sense of a whole life from the attitudes and reactions revealed in a single incident. Anderson said that he got his ideas
from faces he saw as he walked about Chicago. A whole life
history could be seen in a single expression.

Anderson enjoyed his role as father figure to the young
writers, and he took pains to be of as much assistance to
Hemingway as he could. He thought Italy was a poor choice of
destination. There was only one real spot for a writer, and that
was Paris. There was a literary community there, there were
connections to publishing, and it was the most marvelous city in
the world. Hemingway had seen Paris only under Big Bertha's
fire; now he would see it by its own lights.

Hadley adjusted to the change in itinerary. She may have
expected it: Hemingway flew from one enthusiasm to the next
like a hummingbird. She knew he was serious about his writing;
it was the one constant in his life. Now she was also a constant,
and she wondered what effect that would have on him. She
knew of his moods. Hemingway was sometimes serious, sometimes playful; variously modest or full of bluster, the most cheerful person imaginable or deep in a black depression. Occasionally he forgot the pain she still felt over her father's suicide, and

threatened his own. He was not hesitant about displaying his feelings in public, and at more than one party caused her some embarrassment with a display of childish behavior.

Those embarrassing moments always passed, though, and they were not frequent. When he came out of them, laughing, he was once more 'Nesto, or Oin, or Wemedge, lighting her eyes with his smile and her heart with his plans. She loved him as he was, and wouldn't change him for anything. She gave him a new typewriter for what she thought was his twenty-third birthday; she didn't learn until later that he was a year younger than he'd claimed to be.

The wedding date was set for September 3, 1921, with the ceremony to take place at a church near Horton Bay. Hemingway and Hadley could honeymoon at Windemere. Grace and the family were living in the larger house she'd had constructed at Longfield Farm.

Hemingway took a few trout-fishing trips during the summer before his wedding, but he also spent time putting his literary career in shape for the season ahead. He renewed correspondence with newspaper editors he'd met, inquiring as to their interest in occasional freelance pieces from Europe. Cracks were already beginning to appear in the *Cooperative Commonwealth*'s financial foundation, and Hemingway prepared himself to leave the job. He would be quitting soon anyway, taking charge of his own life and work.

Grace took charge of the wedding and more than 400 names accumulated on the invitation list. Hadley's older sister, seeking to take her mother's place in control of Hadley, attempted to warn Hemingway of his fianceé's weakness and frailty. Both Hemingway and Hadley laughed: she was becoming stronger every day. She learned how to kid Hemingway out of his dark moods, and became convinced that he was going to be not only a successful writer but also a great one. They found a small room in Chicago where they would live until embarking for Europe.

One week before the wedding, Hemingway set out for his

last fishing trip of bachelorhood. Hadley, Grace, and the Hemingway sisters scurried through the final preparations for the ceremony, which was set for four o'clock in the afternoon. On their wedding day, both Hadley and Hemingway went for midday swims. Her hair was still damp when she walked down the aisle, but the droplets glowed in the afternoon light and only added to her beauty. That evening Hemingway rowed her across Walloon Lake to Windemere. Their honeymoon lasted two weeks; not even mutual colds could spoil their happiness.

In Chicago that fall, without the support of the *Commonwealth*, Hemingway began to receive responses to his editorial inquiries. The *Toronto Star* was interested in receiving occasional freelance articles—journalistic letters—from Europe, and would pay a good rate. Sherwood Anderson found the young couple temporary lodgings in Paris, and wrote generous letters of introduction to people important to Paris's literary community. Anderson made clear the necessity of knowing the right people: the poet Ezra Pound; James Joyce, the novelist; Gertrude Stein, whose works had influenced Anderson; translator and critic Lewis Galantière. Hemingway already knew many of the names. The prospect of meeting them by introduction was almost too exciting to bear.

Passage was booked for early December. The Hemingways had not acquired much in the way of furniture during their few months of married life, and packing was easy. Hemingway gathered his manuscripts together, carefully stored the letters of introduction, and fastened the case around his typewriter. Hadley, just as excited but more practical, made sure they had plenty of warm clothes, and tried to think of things that would be hard to obtain in France. The night before departure Hemingway gathered all of their canned foods into a large sack and carried them to Sherwood Anderson as a way of saying "thank you."

EIGHT

PARIS

THEY SAILED ON DECEMBER 8, 1921, on the *Leopoldina*. It was not the most comfortable of ships and they were hardly traveling first-class, but the Hemingways had a wonderful voyage. Everything seemed electric and alive. Hemingway was constantly on the go; smiling Hadley hurried to keep up with her husband as he stalked the decks, danced, and spun out his ambitions for hours by the rail. Upon learning of the desperate poverty of a young Frenchwoman and her child, Hemingway applied himself to raising funds for them. A boxing match, he exclaimed, would do the trick, and the charity match was arranged. It lasted three rounds in the dining room and Hemingway was clearly the winner. He shadowboxed up and down the decks.

Their first port of call was Vigo, Spain, where Hemingway was fascinated by the sight of tuna fishermen playing fish that weighed as much as three hundred pounds and were up to six feet long. The prospect of half a dozen giant tuna in the air simultaneously, fishermen bent against their pull, and a Spanish town as backdrop was indelible. Hemingway took it all in.

Vigo was merely a stopping place, though, and tuna fishermen an impressive distraction. The Hemingways arrived in Paris shortly before Christmas and the real adventure began. They checked into the hotel recommended by Sherwood Anderson and were immediately off to explore their new city. Without Big Bertha's shells to capture his attention, Hemingway was free to absorb Paris itself, and he moved nonstop. He seemed almost on the edge of frenzy, nearly desperate to see everything at once. Lewis Galantière had left a note at the hotel inviting the young couple to dinner, and Hemingway managed to contain himself as they ate. Afterward he bubbled over, insisting that he and Galantière spar for a few minutes. The translator could not fend off his new acquaintance's demands, and, though smaller, began trading imaginary punches. Hemingway, dancing, slapping, showing his skill, managed to break Galantière's glasses just hours after they'd met. But he was young, his enthusiasm understandable, his charm unquestionable, and Galantière waved off the blunder. They parted friends.

As Christmas neared, the excitement was tempered by a touch of melancholy. Paris was romantic, but it was also rainy and cold. Their hotel was delightful but they could not afford to stay there long. The apartments they looked at were either filthy or too expensive. On Christmas Day they decided to brighten their spirits with a fine dinner. They walked hand in hand along the streets, pausing to gaze into a restaurant or café, looking for just the right place. At last they selected a small restaurant that was attractive, whose food looked good, and whose prices fit their tight budget. With the meal they had a couple of drinks, toasting each other and Paris. When the bill came, and they saw that they had undercalculated it badly, their festive mood evaporated. Hemingway had to run back to the hotel to fetch more money while Hadley waited, worrying.

Soon things began to brighten. Lewis Galantière, his glasses repaired, helped the Hemingways locate more permanent lodging. They agreed upon a furnished flat at 74, rue du Cardinal Lemoine. The neighborhood was a far cry from Oak Park, and the apartment at number 74 was reached by climbing four flights of stairs that smelled of urine. The room, which served as sleeping as well as living quarters, had a fireplace, but the kitchen and sanitary facilities were minimal. A single toilet, at the head of each flight of stairs, served each floor. At night they could hear accordion music and drunken singing from the dancehall next door. The flat's bed was huge and warm, though, and they could afford the rent. By the New Year they had settled in.

But not for long. Before 1922 was well begun they took their first European holiday, calculating every penny and reckoning that they had enough to afford two weeks in Switzerland. It was exactly what they needed, bright clean air, fumbling attempts at skiing, good food and drink, lovemaking on cold nights, great books by the fire each morning. It cost just a few dollars a day, drove away their homesickness, and renewed in Hemingway his sense of purpose. He had come to Europe to write and it was time to begin.

In Paris he found a room at the top of an old hotel. Its windows looked out on the city; there was a small stove where he could burn twigs for heat and a table at which he could write. The room's finest feature was the solitude it offered him. He could be completely alone in the room, away even from Hadley, concentrating on his work until the rest of the world ceased to exist. The only things in existence were his paper, the pencils that he carefully sharpened, and the words with which he wrestled. He had spoken in Chicago of the novel he planned, and had even begun. On the *Leopoldina,* while Hadley entertained passengers at the piano, Hemingway stared at the sea and tried to imagine the shape his novel would take. Now he was in Paris and his anticipation faded. There was no point in thinking about novels; he was not ready to write a novel. There was not even much point in worrying at stories, for it would take time to be able to complete a whole story. What was important was the sentence—any single sentence, as long as it was simple, free from adornment, and able to capture its subject and fix it on the page clearly for any reader. It had to be *true.*

Often he would leave Hadley sleeping and walk at dawn to the room that served as his office. If he had the money he purchased a bundle of twigs for his stove, but he always glanced at the Parisian chimneys first. His neighbors knew the seasons better than he, and he could not afford to waste money if the chimneys were not drawing. On such days he would wrap a blanket around him against the cold, or if he had the money go to a small café, order coffee, and sip it as he worked. He wrote in notebooks that fit into the pockets of his coat. The notebooks did not fill quickly. It seemed sometimes almost a physical battle, Hemingway against language or at least against language as it had been used until now. He wanted to make something new, to put on the page his experiences but not himself. If he could manage it, the author would not be present at all. Then the reader could come closer to sharing the experience of the story than with any other writer Hemingway had ever read. He thought it was the hardest work imaginable.

In the afternoons, when he was through with writing, he would visit art museums, studying the way Cézanne captured only the most telling elements of a scene. Looking at paintings, he said, helped him learn to write. He began to think that what mattered most in a story might be what was left out. Anderson created whole lives from single incidents, but even Anderson was too wordy, not selective enough. Hemingway's ideas were developing into a theory as he spent long hours over his notebooks or studying paintings.

He was developing social contacts as well. Through his letters from Sherwood Anderson, Hemingway met Ezra Pound, the controversial poet, editor, and literary propagandist. Pound was at the time lobbying for a revolution in prose and poetry, and had worked closely with the poets T. S. Eliot, Wyndham Lewis, and William Butler Yeats as their styles and approaches developed. Pound's own poetry was innovative and difficult, filled with allusions to historical, mythical, and personal incidents and characters. Hemingway at first was put off by Pound's radicalism and fervor. He wrote a parody of Pound, but Lewis Galantière pointed out the foolishness of alienating someone as influential as Pound. Hemingway paid the poet further visits and grew to like him. Soon he was giving Ezra Pound instruction in boxing and self-defense.

Hemingway and Hadley were too poor to purchase books,

but they had learned of a private lending library that rented books for a small fee. Following work one day, Hemingway stopped by the crowded library and marveled at the long shelves of books, the photographs of writers that filled every wall. Sylvia Beach, who owned the library, introduced herself to Hemingway, and told him to feel free to select as many books as he wanted. Her library, Shakespeare and Company, was a gathering place for English and American writers in Paris. All the expatriates met there for conversation and books. Hemingway did not have the money to pay the rental deposit, but Sylvia Beach waved away his objections. She was charmed by him; he could stop by with the money later. He selected *A Sportsman's Sketches* by Turgenev and a novel by D. H. Lawrence. When Sylvia insisted that he take more to read he chose *War and Peace* and Dostoevski's *The Gambler*. That evening he brought Hadley by, paid the deposit, and spoke with Sylvia while Hadley made her choice among the works of the novelist Henry James.

Perhaps the most important of Hemingway's literary friends was Gertrude Stein, an American who had lived in Paris since before World War I. She had studied psychology with William James, she was a homosexual, and she was fascinated with the processes by which people thought. She was a more formal experimentalist than Hemingway or Pound, seeking to write prose and poetry that approximated thought. Her work often made little intellectual sense and was difficult to read objectively. Gertrude Stein was a lesbian who had written frankly of her sexual bias and was still controversial. Her apartment was a true salon, where artists and writers gathered to listen to her pronouncements on art and literature. While Ernest listened to Gertrude Stein, Hadley had tea with Stein's lover and companion, Alice B. Toklas. Sometimes on the way home the young couple would joke about the two fierce-looking women.

Ezra Pound and Gertrude Stein were serious in their approach and dedication to literature, just as Sylvia Beach and Lewis Galantière were committed to its support. Hemingway met James Joyce, whose novel *Ulysses*, just published, was already recognized as one of the major novels of the period. Its reputation and importance would grow, and Hemingway was in awe of Joyce's enormous achievement. Joyce pursued an ambition not unlike Gertrude Stein's: he wanted to capture thought on paper. In *Ulysses* he had succeeded, capturing twenty-four hours in the life of Dubliner Leopold Bloom and fashioning of that single day not only a book that made real Bloom's entire life, but also the lives of his wife and others, and something like a myth for the modern world. *Ulysses* was an enormous book, but not a word was wasted. Through interior monologue—stream of consciousness—he put down sentences that were clearer approximations of the thought process than even Gertrude Stein's. Even more important, Joyce's work was readable to the point of being difficult to put down. Hemingway's enthusiasm for Joyce was unstoppable, but he had learned a great deal about literary politics from Lewis Galantière. Perhaps because he had succeeded more fully than she, James Joyce's work and name were anathema to Gertrude Stein; so Hemingway kept his friendships separate.

There was an artistic revolution going on in Paris, and it, like all such revolutions, attracted followers and pretenders. Nearly every café and bar was lined with young men and women, dressed as rough bohemians, talking passionately of the work they were going to do, drinking themselves senseless over such talk, and then rising to talk more. Hemingway quickly saw through such posturing and would have nothing to do with the phonies. He wrote a piece for the *Toronto Star Weekly* about these would-be artists, claiming that the worst scum from Greenwich Village's artistic community had been transplanted to Paris. Nothing made him more furious than to be interrupted at serious work in a café by a scruffy expatriate who wanted to talk about writing, not do it. When that happened the creative mood he worked so hard to build simply collapsed.

As their marriage grew older, Hadley began to see patterns

in her husband's depressions. He would go for days or weeks with his head down, unable to articulate his problems, snapping at her and everyone else he encountered. He would never be a writer and perhaps it was time to give up the dream. Then he would one afternoon come home from his office, bound up the four flights of stairs as though they were one, and sweep her into his arms and into a mood of joy, laughing and singing loudly that he would be a writer, that nothing could stop him. Hadley believed this and believed in him. His dedication to writing was complete, his fits of ecstasy sometimes triggered by a single sentence he'd written.

As the Paris winter began showing signs of turning to spring, Hemingway applied himself to building sentences into paragraphs, and thus into stories. In Michigan he had written of a gangsters' restaurant in Chicago: "When you enter the room, and you have no more chance than the zoological entrant in the famous camel-needle's eye gymkana of entering the room unless you are approved . . . a varying number of eyes will look you over with that detached intensity that comes of a periodic contemplation of death." The story was only two years old but it seemed to Hemingway to be nothing but words, too many words too carelessly chosen. In Paris he began to write about Michigan.

He sat at his desk and thought of what he knew to be true, looking through his memories and experiences for moments that could be transformed into fiction. He did not write of the war yet. He thought of Liz Dilworth's restaurant, of Horton Bay, of the lakeside loss of his virginity to one of Liz's waitresses. It all began to come together. If he was going to break new stylistic ground, he would also break ground in terms of honesty and approach to sex. "Jim Gilmore came to Horton Bay from Canada," he wrote, a simple sentence. "He bought the blacksmith shop from old man Horton. Jim was short and dark with big mustaches and big hands."

He took Liz Dilworth's first name for his female character.

"Liz Coates worked for Smith's . . . Liz had good legs and always wore clean gingham aprons and Jim noticed that her hair was always neat behind." Hemingway wanted his sentences to establish mood as well as information. He used the pages of his notebooks to work out experiments with language, eliminating any artificiality, any intrusion by the author.

"Liz liked Jim very much. She liked it the way he walked over from the shop. . . . She liked it about how white his teeth were when he smiled. She liked it very much that he didn't look like a blacksmith." Rhythm and repetition, patterns of words and emphases, the arrangement of paragraphs on a page—everything contributed to the mood.

The work continued to go slowly, but he found that he could use his new techniques to build tension, bringing Jim and Liz together until his rough seduction of her becomes inevitable. He could show thoughts, opening the reader to both Liz and Jim, and then focusing upon Liz. Perhaps best of all was the way the style could convey action, releasing all of the tension in a few sharp sentences. Then the story came to a close. "She walked over to the edge of the dock and looked down to the water. There was a mist coming up from the bay. She was cold and miserable and everything felt gone. . . . A cold mist was coming up through the woods from the bay."

He called the story "Up in Michigan." It was something new, and Gertrude Stein appreciated the level of craft and control that it had required. But she had no use for the story's brutality, because that rendered "Up in Michigan" unpublishable. Hemingway had wanted publication badly, but suddenly he was in no hurry for it. Many of the pieces he wrote, because of their subject matter or form, were automatically unpublishable in existing markets. Ernest Hemingway knew that as he composed them. Next to the work itself, the markets were of no concern. He was trying to make something new, and once it was well made there would be a market for it.

That spring his journalism was being published regularly:

nearly thirty pieces were accepted by the *Toronto Star,* a daily paper, and the *Toronto Star Weekly.* When writing as a journalist, Hemingway was scrupulous about his market. He shaped his prose to a newspaper's needs, making his own interests interesting to the readership. In the *Star* he deliberately introduced himself as guide, showing the hotels of Switzerland as he'd seen them, paying homage to Vigo and its tuna fishermen, mocking the bohemians and poseurs. His editors noticed his growing skill and range, and assigned Hemingway to cover an important economic conference in Genoa. It was his first trip to Italy since the war. He traveled without Hadley and spent his time working hard. He filed more than two dozen pieces, further establishing himself with his editors. Hemingway's journalistic career looked promising. He was wounded once more as well, when a hot water heater exploded and several pieces of metal struck him as he bathed; the *Star* mentioned the accident on page five.

Journalism was not lucrative, but Hemingway's abilities as a political correspondent allowed him to file more than simply travel and human interest pieces. Between his articles and Hadley's trust, they managed not only to get by but also to take occasional trips. They went on all-day outings to the horse races, betting carefully, planning exuberant evenings with their winnings. Hemingway's fascination with boxing deepened in Paris, and he often shadowboxed through the cobblestone streets. He claimed that the boxing reports and the horse race reports he read helped him master French. He and Hadley practiced their French on long walks through the countryside.

By May they had saved enough money for a longer trip, and Hemingway insisted that he show Hadley Italy. It was a wonderful plan, and included a visit with Eric Dorman-Smith, whom they met in the mountains for skiing. Chink, still a professional soldier, had not changed, and he and Hemingway renewed their friendship immediately. They agreed that they would all hike through the St. Bernard Pass into Italy, and they were soon knee-keep in snow, with Hadley's simple walking shoes splitting and her feet badly blistered. They took shelter in a monastery where Hadley, despite her discomfort, wandered through the stone building, unknowingly violating the monks' quarters with her female presence. Such a thing had not happened in ten centuries and it was something for the three of them to laugh about as they completed—by train—their journey to Italy.

Hemingway did not stop working during the trip. He arranged an interview with Benito Mussolini. He took notes and reported intelligently on Italy's shift to the political right. He took advantage of occasional stops to fish new rivers and then write articles comparing European trout fishing to American. Hadley took up a fly rod and found her husband a wonderful teacher. She was excited by the prospect of seeing Fossalta, where he had been wounded. It was no sentimental journey, for as Hemingway discovered and reported in the *Star,* Fossalta had been repaired and rebuilt. Every reminder of the war had been covered with new plaster or bright paint. Nothing, it seemed to him, had been learned, nothing gained from the thousands of deaths on the banks of the Piave.

The effects of the war were all around and Hemingway noticed them all. He and Hadley traveled through Germany, fishing and living royally on a few cents a day thanks to the collapse of the German economy. In his dispatches Hemingway captured the frustration of the Germans, the desperate tension that exploded into violent riots, the Belgians' rabid hatred of the Germans. His articles were tightly written and evocative, some of them effectively short stories capturing the mood of a defeated nation. When he tired of political and economic stories, he shifted to outdoor pieces full of excellent expert instruction on how to camp and obtain permission to fish in Europe. Even in these articles, though, Hemingway was attentive to the political and emotional atmosphere.

In September he received his chance to return to real rather than remembered war when the *Star* ordered him to Constantinople to report on the conflict between the Greeks and the Turks. Kemal Ataturk's organized Turkish resistance had grown into an effective army that had routed the Greeks at Smyrna. Hemingway arrived in Constantinople near the end of the month, after a four-day train journey. The city was filthy and full of fear; Hemingway soon found himself covered with lice and shivering with malaria. Although working under contract for the *Star*, he was moonlighting as a freelance journalist for a wire service. In effect, he was covering the same news twice. Hemingway had not been in Constantinople long before he received a telegram from the offices of the *Star* remarking on the similarity between his dispatches and those which came over the wires. He worked harder to make his *Star* stories more original. When he had the strength he went outside and watched with amazement and horror as tens of thousands of Greeks fled from the approaching Turks. He tried to take in every face, seeing suffering and misery to a degree not witnessed even on the battlefields of Italy.

The violence and fear fascinated Hemingway but his energy was gone. During the days he sought newspaper stories, at night he searched for clean blankets with which to wrap himself as the malaria wracked him. He remained in Turkey for more than three weeks, returning to Paris in late October, sick, infested to the point of having to have his head shaved, and exhausted. He and Hadley had quarreled bitterly before he departed. She had not wanted him to go, and from a refugee he had bought her a present: two beautiful necklaces. Best of all, the trip had earned him enough money to allow him to write nothing but fiction for a while.

Sherwood Anderson's letters of introduction and Lewis Galantière's guidance through the delicate world of literary politics were beginning to pay off. The established artists and patrons in Paris knew Hemingway now, recognized his talent and his ferocious discipline and dedication. They helped him place a few poems for publication in the United States, one of them appearing opposite the work of another young veteran, William

Faulkner. Hemingway placed several poems that year in small magazines, but his inclination and his gift were for prose. He worked at several sketches—not stories, but not fragments either. He rendered brief descriptions of people he'd met, things he'd seen. Sometimes they were satiric, sometimes bitter and horrifying. In each sketch he tried to sharpen his technique, reducing always the amount of description and comment.

Hemingway was working on one full-bodied story as well. He set the story at the racetracks he and Hadley had come to love, and told the story through the voice of a young boy whose father was a jockey. "My Old Man" was the longest story he'd undertaken yet, and it challenged his craft in many ways. Because the story was in the first person, Hemingway had to make its observations match those of his narrator, Joe. Because Joe was young, Hemingway had to catch the rhythm of youthful language on the page. It was quite a test of his theory of fiction, and when the story was finished Hemingway's pride was enormous. "My Old Man," he and Hadley thought, was the sort of story that could begin to create a real reputation for Ernest Hemingway.

He took the story with him when he traveled to Lausanne to report on the peace conference between the Greeks and the Turks. Again, in order to make money, Hemingway was serving wire news agencies as well as the *Star*. Despite his heavy load he was eager to mingle with other journalists at the conference, hopeful of getting an editor to read "My Old Man."

The conference dragged on and by early December he wanted Hadley to join him. She agreed to come to Lausanne by train and planned a special surprise for her husband. Because she knew how much he hated being away from his real work, she carefully packed into a satchel his manuscripts, stories, fragments, and poetry, plus the new novel he was beginning, to present to Hemingway upon her arrival. It would be a wonderful surprise. She treated herself to a taxi to the train station. Hadley stopped to buy a newspaper to read during the trip to

Lausanne and when she turned back to her luggage the satchel containing her husband's work was gone. She looked up and down the station but could not find the satchel or any sign of the thief who'd stolen it.

There was nothing to be done; she took her seat on the train to Lausanne. No matter how hard she tried, she could not imagine anything worse than what had happened. She understood that Hemingway's work was the center of his life, even more than she was, and she could not imagine how he would react to the news.

He was waiting for her at the station in Lausanne, and he knew immediately that something was wrong. When Hadley told him of the theft Hemingway put on a brave face to cheer her up. It was bad, he said, but he was a professional and kept carbon copies of all his work. Hadley was afraid she had packed the carbons as well, but Hemingway said that was impossible. He took a train to Paris immediately, to gather his carbons and assure his wife that all was not lost. But all of his work *had* been lost: Hadley had packed the carbons as well as the originals. Everything was gone.

For a while he sat in the apartment. It was hard to know what to do. He knew how hard he had worked on the stories, what he had attempted to create, what he had accomplished. There seemed little hope of getting the manuscripts back: a thief, finding the papers valueless, would have destroyed them by now. The thought of all that work destroyed sickened Hemingway. He could not sit in the apartment long. He never told anyone what he did during the night of the loss, but by the next morning he had adopted a demeanor of cynical humor. He laughed bitterly about his manuscripts, returned to Lausanne for the end of the peace conference, and took Hadley to the Swiss mountains for Christmas skiing. It was a way of trying to get over the tragedy. Chink Dorman-Smith joined the Hemingways, and there was also a visit from an old Oak Park neighbor.

The holiday mood, Hadley smiling once more, friends—

none of them could make up for the emptiness Hemingway felt. Although he occasionally put pencil to paper for a brief poem, or even a line or two of prose, Hemingway's will to work, the discipline of which he was so proud, had been shattered. It was as if the theft of his manuscripts revealed to him how perishable talent was, how easily his gift could disappear. He told more than one person that he was through with writing forever.

Hemingway and Hadley left Switzerland in early 1923, traveling to Rapallo, Italy, where Ezra Pound had established an artistic outpost to escape the Parisian winter. Perhaps the Mediterranean would brighten his mood. Before they left Switzerland, Hadley told Ernest that she was pregnant, and although he feigned happiness he was aware of the ways in which a child would change his life. For the time being he was free from the pressures of journalism—with a child to feed his vacations from reporting would be fewer. The freedom of the expatriate artist was far different from the responsibilities of the family man, and he wondered how those responsibilities would affect his writing.

For a while in Rapallo he sought simply to relax, seeing to it that Hadley enjoyed herself. He treated her to a lovely dinner to celebrate her pregnancy. He continued to joke about the loss of his manuscripts. Hemingway listened to Ezra Pound holding forth on literature and on the historical sources of his poetic allusions. A new friend, Mike Strater, joined them, painting a portrait of Hadley and frequently sparring for exercise with Hemingway.

Despite his pretense that he was through with writing, Hemingway remained eager to speak with editors. He learned that Edward O'Brien was living in Rapallo and paid a call. At thirty-two O'Brien was a published poet, but more important, he combed each year's magazines for stories worthy of inclusion in the *Best Short Stories* volume he edited annually. O'Brien and Hemingway got along well, and O'Brien seemed nearly as pained by Hemingway's loss as the author himself. Hemingway showed O'Brien "My Old Man," which had been under submission when Hadley packed the satchel, and which along with "Up in Michigan" was all that remained of his work. O'Brien promised to read the story.

Soon he was promising more. O'Brien's collections were assembled from magazines, but the editor knew right away that "My Old Man" was something special. He told Hemingway that he wanted to make an exception to the rules. Because of the author's control of his material, because of the story's pace, its style and substance, O'Brien intended to include "My Old Man" by Ernest Hemingway in *The Best Short Stories of 1923*, and would even dedicate the volume to Hemingway.

Hemingway at last seemed to come alive. His excitement was as intense as had been his depression. He bounded through the streets, energetic, charged with purpose and plans. Even Ezra Pound's lengthy lectures concerning obscure historical figures became interesting. More interesting still were Pound's plans for a series of small books that Pound would edit and arrange to have published. The books would show the best work of the best new writers, and Pound hoped one of the books would be by Ernest Hemingway.

After leaving Rapallo, Hemingway and Hadley lingered in Italy, first on a long hike with the Pounds, then going to Cortina to ski. Hemingway still had funds from his stint as a reporter in Lausanne, there was the income from Hadley's trust fund, and the two could live cheaply in Italy. He resumed regular hours at his desk, rediscovering his enthusiasm for his work, reestablishing his discipline. He struggled with several sketches. The pieces were brief and self-contained, Hemingway's renderings of incidents he'd seen or heard about in Europe or America. Often they were sharp violent moments captured in absolutely clear sentences. He gave some of the pieces chapter numerals, as though they were part of a novel; others had titles as though they were short stories. He tried to write them as

carefully and tightly as he would a newspaper story to be trans-
mitted by telegraph.

Hemingway had to break off from his literary work once
more to take a journalistic assignment. In March 1923, the *Star*
sent him to Germany to cover the deepening tensions caused by
the recent French occupation of the Ruhr. Hadley remained in
Cortina; when Hemingway returned the thaw would be over
and they could fish.

The scenery of the Ruhr attracted Hemingway from the
moment he arrived: he appreciated the beauty of the Black
Forest, the cleanliness of the German towns, the rich plains on
the banks of the Rhine. But he also appreciated the bitterness of
the Germans over the occupation by French and Belgian troops.
The Ruhr was Germany's leading mining and manufacturing
region, and the French had seized it because of Germany's inability to pay fully the reparations assessed them as part of the
Armistice. The German government demanded a French with-
drawal, but was helpless to back up its demands. The League of
Nations, to which an appeal was presented, found itself impo-
tent against French determination.

Hemingway's dispatches caught, through careful reporting
not only of political situations but also of character and indi-
vidual incidents, the hatred and frustration of the Germans. He
attacked the French press, and reported that the occupation was
not succeeding in winning for France any financial gain—its only
success was in building a foundation of German hostility from
which some bitter future would rise.

The Ruhr pieces showed Hemingway as a fully matured and
professional journalist. His stories were crisp, newsworthy, and
effective. He was more than living up to the promise he had
shown. Toronto readers were even treated in one issue to a
profile of Hemingway along with a story by him: the reporter
was nearly as newsworthy as the events he covered.

The journalistic promise, however, grew increasingly difficult for Hemingway to keep. He was weary of reporting, resentful of the time it took away from his fiction—the writing he considered his only real work. Despite the fact that his dispatches earned money vital for their support, Hemingway told Hadley more than once that he wanted to abandon reporting altogether. He would never know, he argued, how important a writer he could become unless he gave himself to his craft completely and without compromise. He told others, too, and Gertrude Stein encouraged him to follow his brave talk with brave action. But talk was all Hemingway could afford: as Hadley's pregnancy became more obvious it became also a constant reminder of the responsibilities that loomed ahead. Starvation for art might be a fine credo for an artist, but there were other lives involved now. Even as he talked of writing fiction full-time, he was making plans to return to Canada with Hadley for the birth of their child. He arranged for a job with the *Toronto Star,* and talked of staying in North America for two years or so, saving money for their next trip to Europe.

Hemingway could take comfort, at least, in the improvement in his writing since he and Hadley had come to Europe. There was physical evidence of that improvement as well. By early summer of 1923, plans were under way for publication of two books by Ernest Hemingway. An acquaintance, Robert McAlmon, was convinced of Hemingway's importance as a writer, and wanted to publish a limited-edition collection of Hemingway's stories and poems. It would be Ernest Hemingway's first book, and Hemingway set about assembling its contents. Despite his renewed enthusiasm and productivity, there was not a great deal of material from which to choose. He had the short stories "My Old Man," "Up in Michigan," and "Out of Season"—a new one, written in Cortina following the trip to the Ruhr. Hemingway also had in hand ten poems; on occasion he had introduced himself as a poet. The short stories, though, showed his talent most clearly, and they would be the heart of the collection.

Ezra Pound's plans to publish Hemingway were also proceeding, placing Hemingway in the position of having two books in preparation without sufficient material to fill them. Day after day he stayed at his desk for hours, working on sketches in which he tried further to distill the techniques he had mastered as a reporter. Occasionally he spoke of the theory behind his fiction, explaining that he wanted to achieve dramatic effects on the page by leaving out material other writers might consider the most important parts of their pieces. In his short stories he might accomplish this effect by structuring a story around the events leading up to a suicide, and then leaving out the suicide: it did not matter; the mood and tension were all there on the page. In the sketches his method was even more severe and his approach was more distant: here he included only the climax of what might have been a long story or even a novel. The sketches were sharp moments that captured almost photographically time and place, terror and courage, death and despair. Few of them were more than a hundred words long.

During the summer of 1923, with both book publication and a return to Canada and domestic duties ahead of him, Hemingway made time in the midst of his work for a few last trips. He was lately fascinated with Spain and traveled there twice, once with Hadley. On the other trip he accompanied a good crew of friends, a gang every bit as much as those on the Michigan trout trips. The Spanish atmosphere was ideal for such companionship. Hemingway was much taken by the bullfight, and by the ritual which surrounded and informed it, and he was quick to chide those of his friends who found it horrifying. Bullfights were enveloped in a celebratory air for which the Spanish had a word: *fiesta.* There was much drunkenness and singing, late hours and early rising, an almost desperate revelry revolving around an event at whose heart was death. That was the center that captured Hemingway's attention: the death of the bull, the possibility of the matador's death. It was not random death such as he had witnessed on the battlefield, but a ceremony of death possessing its own strict code of behavior and courage in which the approach to death followed a formal and stately pattern. Even two brief exposures to Spain and the bullfight marked Hemingway; he incorporated some of what he had seen into material for the book of sketches.

By August they were packing for the return to Canada. Hemingway had a few last conferences with Ezra Pound, going over the eighteen sketches that would make up the book. It would be published later in the year and would be called *in our time*, the lowercase being one more representation of Hemingway's attempt to break down barriers and chip away at traditions. The proofs of the book to be published by Robert McAlmon, *Three Stories and Ten Poems*, arrived shortly before the Hemingways sailed for Canada. If the book was a symbol of how far Hemingway had come as a writer during his time in Paris, its brevity could also be seen as a reminder of how far he had to go. Its title was still very nearly an inventory of Ernest Hemingway's work!

But there was new work coming, and there would be more new work after the baby was old enough to come to Paris. Two years . . . it was not so long, really. It was longer, though, than he and Hadley had stayed in Europe. How much he had changed since then. The energetic and boyish newlywed who had bounded through the streets of Paris was now a confident young man. His features had filled out and people could feel the power of his body and his personality simply by glancing at him. The mustache with which he had flirted since adolescence was now a permanent part of his face, defining his character as well as his features—bold, strong, dark. He was twenty-four years old and would shortly have two books published. He was well known in the Parisian artistic community. He was attracting attention for the simplicity of his style and his ability to control it. He was a writer of great promise, returning to America to support a wife and child. Everything would be all right.

Hemingway and Hadley arrived in Canada late in August

1923, and it soon became clear that everything was not going to be all right. They settled into an apartment infinitely more comfortable than the one they'd had in Paris, and after months of scrimping for pennies Hemingway's salary of $125 a week seemed like royal wages. But Toronto was not Paris, and the role of reporter for the *Star* was far different from the role of roving correspondent.

Despite Hemingway's salary and credentials, his new editor, Harry Hindmarsh, assigned him to the same sorts of stories he'd covered in Kansas City: the police beat, the hospitals, escaped convicts. Hemingway was at first given no by-line. Hindmarsh had little use for reporters who were celebrities, and less use, it seemed, for reporters who fancied themselves serious journalists. Hemingway was treated as an apprentice and, although he managed to write a few feature stories about European scenery and sport, few of the assignments he received were challenging or interesting.

Hemingway tried to put his frustrations aside for Hadley's sake. The baby was due in early October, and they tried to concentrate on that, looking for diversions to keep their minds off the unfortunate, unfair situation at the *Star*. They visited old Toronto friends, and Hemingway became friends with some younger writers. When the first copies of *Three Stories and Ten Poems* arrived there was a celebration, and Hemingway went quickly to work sending copies to influential reviewers.

Hindmarsh was not satisfied simply to put the young reporter through the humiliation of stories without by-lines. It seemed as though the editor looked for ways to try Hemingway's patience, sending him out of town to cover a story about mining and then, as Hadley's delivery date neared, assigning Hemingway to cover the visit of David Lloyd George, Britain's Prime Minister, to New York. Hemingway protested—his child was due almost immediately. Hindmarsh was unyielding, and ordered Hemingway to New York. Though his impulse may have been to rebel, Hemingway could not forget how important the job and paycheck were to his family. He packed his bags and told Hadley to be brave. He would be back before the baby was born.

He was on his way back to Toronto on October 10 when Hadley gave birth to a seven-pound, five-ounce boy, whom they named John Hadley Nicanor Hemingway. Nicanor was chosen out of respect for a matador whose technique Hemingway greatly admired. The birth went easily, but the father's life was complicated once more by work. As though it had not been bad enough to miss the actual delivery, Hemingway made Hindmarsh furious by going first to the hospital rather than to the newspaper office. Hemingway took the dressing-down stoically, bragging to his friends among the reporters that he would have his revenge when he became an important writer.

He was doing very little writing, though, and the two years seemed to stretch out like a prison term. Both the baby and Hadley were healthy, but Hemingway was beginning to show signs of strain. To commit himself to a job in order to support a family was one thing; to spend his time on meaningless stories that not only did nothing for his journalistic career but also, he believed, did harm to his talent for serious writing, was another. Hemingway wanted to be in Paris and he began to talk to Hadley of returning more quickly than they had planned.

The *Star* had been good to him, though, and he called upon the managing editor, John Bone, for assistance in dealing with Hindmarsh's demands. The *Star* offered too much security for Hemingway to surrender without seriously attempting to salvage the situation. He had worked with Bone before, and managed to place a few articles about bullfights with the *Star Weekly*. They were small comfort.

At least there were greater comforts at home. The baby was a delight, taking great pleasure, as Hemingway wrote to his father, in squalling constantly. Hadley had come through the delivery well, baby John gained weight quickly, and it was a pleasure for Hemingway to be financially able to secure a nurse to help Hadley. They adjusted easily to the routines imposed by parenthood, and Hemingway wrote proud letters to Gertrude Stein, Ezra Pound, Sylvia Beach, and other friends from Paris. Accompanying his fatherly pride, however, was bitterness over the loss of freedom he experienced because of the demands of his work and his editor. He could feel his spirit dwindling, and by the middle of November, barely two months after returning to Canada, he knew that staying in Canada was not going to work.

Shortly before Christmas 1923, Hemingway traveled to Oak Park to visit his parents. He did not linger long, telling his family only that their grandchild was doing fine and that the baby's father would soon be making a change in his life. His mind was made up. Security was fine, and it was important for some people, but too great a desire for security was the enemy of art. He was an artist and he was going to do great work, and there was no weekly check large enough to pay for the loss of that work. He wrote Sylvia Beach and asked her to find an apartment for the Hemingways. It would not be so nice as their Toronto home, for he intended to do no more journalism. That was hackwork, even at its best falling far short of what he could achieve as a writer of fiction.

He made one last attempt to come to terms with Hindmarsh, but when that failed he sat down at his typewriter to compose his own declaration of independence. "I regret very much," he wrote, "the necessity of tendering my resignation from the local staff of the Star. This resignation to take effect January 1st, 1924 if convenient to you.

"Please believe there is no rudeness implied through the brevity of this memorandum."

It was December 27, 1923. Ernest Hemingway was through with journalism as a career. He was taking his family back to Paris, where they would be poor but where he could learn how to become a great writer.

NINE

SUNRISE

THEY ARRIVED IN PARIS in January 1924, and to Hemingway it was a genuine homecoming. This city was where he lived and worked. He, Hadley, and the baby settled into an apartment at 113, rue Notre Dame des Champs that was larger, more comfortable, and more sanitary than had been their flat on rue du Cardinal Lemoine. The new apartment overlooked a sawmill whose whine, no matter how reminiscent of the Indian camp at Walloon Lake, became a distraction to Hemingway, who found other places to do his writing.

Their lives quickly settled into a routine. Finances were tight, the Hemingways having gone from a reporter's salary of $125 a week to a monthly budget of approximately $100. Too soon they found the income from Hadley's trust fund reduced. In an attempt to increase its yield they had placed its principal in the hands of a friend whose counsel proved poor. Bad investments led to the principal's being cut in half, and there were weeks when the Hemingways had no money at all.

Despite the financial pressures, though, their new start in Paris was a happy time for the Hemingways. Their baby was a delight, the center of their lives, and Hemingway as always began to search for a suitable nickname. Although for a while he referred to the infant as the "young Gallito," he soon settled upon "Bumby," and the name stuck. Hemingway rose early to prepare Bumby's morning feeding, working efficiently with bottles and nipples, making an occasional note for a story, holding the child as Bumby ate. A cat, Feather Puss, wandered through the apartment as Hemingway fed Bumby. The scent of cedar and the song of the sawmill filled the air. As morning deepened Hemingway would play with Bumby, teaching the child early to ball his fists and make scary faces. When Bumby did not seem to be gaining weight as quickly as he should, Hemingway invited the poet William Carlos Williams to visit the apartment. Williams, who was by profession a physician, prescribed nothing more for Bumby than solid food, and on his new diet Bumby began to grow at a satisfying rate.

When Hadley awoke, Hemingway left the apartment to find a quiet spot in which to work. He knew that Paris was full of people who had left America with plans to become great writers, and who now did nothing. He had no intention of following their example. The abandonment of journalism seemed to have opened his creative resources more fully than ever before. He had more ideas for stories than he could handle. He drew upon his childhood, remembering Walloon Lake, the tension between his parents, his own sense of being out of place when he returned to Oak Park after the war. Writing came no more quickly than it ever had for Hemingway, but now it came constantly. With no journalistic assignments to interrupt him, he forced himself into the rhythm of daily work. His ability with simple declarative sentences, his theories regarding the implication of dramatic events rather than their presentation, and his desire to put the truth of experience on the printed page were all being put to a severe, disciplined test.

As he worked at his stories he also sought to solidify his position within Paris's literary community. He continued to meet with Gertrude Stein, was a frequent patron of Sylvia Beach's Shakespeare and Company, spoke occasionally with James Joyce, and listened to Ezra Pound hold forth. Many noticed that Hemingway looked more like a longshoreman than a writer, with his muscular frame, thick mustache, and tattered tennis shoes. The shoes' condition was a reflection of Hemingway's poverty as much as of his disregard for social niceties.

Other artists' dress was more calculated. Hemingway's opinion of most of the undiscovered writers in Paris was unchanged: he had no use for the phonies who wore rags to proclaim their dedication to art. Whatever art they had was practiced over endless glasses at any number of bars. Still, he moved with some frequency among the bohemians, drinking with them, watching them, mocking them at the same time he measured his performance and career against their empty talk.

The phonies came to Paris because Paris attracted serious artists, and Hemingway made a point of meeting the sincere young writers as well as the pretenders. He renewed his acquaintance with John Dos Passos, who was now working on a novel called *Manhattan Transfer,* seeking to adapt some of the techniques of the cinema to the medium of prose. Archibald MacLeish, a poet, became a friend, as did Donald Ogden Stewart, a humorist. A young novelist named Harold Loeb fascinated Hemingway. At thirty-three Loeb was nearly nine years older than Hemingway, but he seemed much younger, more naive. Hemingway could not tell if Loeb was serious about writing, or merely another phony.

Ezra Pound introduced Hemingway to Ford Madox Ford. Ford was fifty-two, and had embarked upon his linked quartet of novels, *Parade's End,* although he was best known as a critic and editor. Ford was not universally liked, and his career as a novelist had not met with great success. Although they were of different temperaments and inclinations—Ford at first thought Hemingway's energy a sign of frenzy—Ford and Hemingway established close ties. Ford had come to Paris to start a little magazine, *transatlantic review,* in which he intended to print the finest and most experimental works of contemporary writers. Hemingway came quickly to serve as Ford's assistant editor, and although he received no salary he put in long hours and accepted increasing responsibility for the magazine's contents. He worked closely with Gertrude Stein, helping her prepare an excerpt from her manuscript *The Making of Americans.* Hemingway helped Ford with the layout and arrangement of the first issue, which included a portion of the novel James Joyce would eventually call *Finnegans Wake,* and a short story called "Indian Camp," by Ernest Hemingway.

"Indian Camp" was one of the stories Hemingway had written earlier in the year, a story in which he drew upon his childhood, his memories, his father. It focused upon Nick Adams, a young boy on a fishing trip in Michigan with his father, who is a physician, and his uncle. Dr. Adams is called at dawn to deliver a baby at the Indian camp, and he takes his son with him to see the birth. Hemingway worried over the story, cutting it, revising it until the reader could see its scenes as clearly as Nick experienced them.

"Inside on a wooden bunk lay a young Indian woman. She had been trying to have her baby for two days. All the old women in the camp had been helping her. The men had moved off up the road to sit in the dark and smoke out of range of the noise she made. She screamed just as Nick and the two Indians followed his father and Uncle George into the shanty. She lay in the lower bunk, very big under a quilt. Her head was turned to one side. In the upper bunk was her husband. He had cut his foot very badly with an ax three days before. He was smoking a pipe. The room smelled very bad."

Throughout the story, which is barely seven pages long, Hemingway holds Nick at the center. "Indian Camp" unfolds around Nick Adams, allowing the reader to share the boy's thoughts and see the things the boy sees. Although he did not leave out the climax of this story—the suicide of the baby's father at the moment his wife is in greatest pain—Hemingway also did not dwell upon it. It was simply one more detail, a piece among other pieces, filtered through Nick Adams by a young and still generally unpublished young writer who was becoming a master of clean, clear prose.

Ford Madox Ford, among others, understood that the simplicity of Hemingway's language belied the complexity of the young man's art and the intensity with which he worked at it. Ford thought Hemingway was already one of the great prose stylists of the generation and proclaimed a brilliant future for him. Hemingway's stories, though, continued to come back, and their author found himself from time to time earning a few necessary francs as a sparring partner for aspiring boxers.

At the same time, he was beginning to look for an American publisher for a collection of short stories. He thought that his new pieces could be added to those in *Three Stories,* with the sketches from *in our time* appearing between longer pieces to make a good book. Boni and Liveright, Sherwood Anderson's publisher, expressed very cautious interest in such a collection, and Hemingway applied himself with even more dedication and determination to new stories.

By summer 1924, he had finished several, some of them offering further glimpses of Nick Adams at various stages of his life. Each in its own way, the stories were about the nature of courage, with the events described being incidents from which Nick's education in bravery and manhood were derived. "The Doctor and the Doctor's Wife" showed Nick's father again, in confrontation with the Indians who lived near his summer home, attempting to prove his courage but prevented by his wife, a pious woman who allowed no breach of Christian decorum. It was a devastating story. "The Three-Day Blow," "The End of Something," and "Cross-Country Snow" presented Nick learning to drink liquor, having his first romance, skiing in Europe. There were hints in some of the stories that Nick wanted to become a writer.

Not all of the stories Hemingway undertook dealt with Nick Adams. "Mr. and Mrs. Elliot" and "Cat in the Rain" re-created the experiences of Americans in Europe. "Soldier's Home" told the story of Krebs, a young man whose return from the First World War was marked by the tension between the veteran and his family, especially his mother. Hemingway put into each sentence of the story the explosive frustration of an adolescent who had come back from war changed, unable to explain how, unable to convince his mother that he could no longer play the obedient, God-fearing role she wanted most for him. It was a genuinely painful story—Hemingway was using his art to come to terms with his life.

The good season's work of early 1924 deserved a holiday, and in early summer Hemingway began to plan a trip to Spain. The bullfighting season was nearly under way and he would not miss it. Hemingway had first to deal with his editorial responsibilities at *transatlantic review,* as Ford put the contents of the August issue entirely in Hemingway's hands. Hemingway called upon Dos Passos and other friends for material already available so that they might more quickly be off to the bullfights. He left the August issue in the hands of the printer, Bumby in the care of a nursemaid, and with Hadley, Dos Passos, Chink Dorman-Smith, and others set out in early July for several weeks of bullfighting, carousing, and trout fishing in Spain.

It was a wonderful and exciting holiday. Hemingway studied each bullfight carefully, attempting to understand completely the meaning of the ceremony, the technical and symbolic nature of the action and the drama. He took notes, spoke with matadors, and even revealed his own courage by confronting a bull or two, although the bulls he faced had padded horns. Each day he added to his knowledge, practiced his skill. *Aficionado* was the Spanish word for one who fully understood the bullfight, and to become an *aficionado* was increasingly among Hemingway's ambitions.

The holiday over, he returned to his literary ambitions, and soon found himself immersed in the longest story he'd yet attempted. He called it "Big Two-Hearted River" and it was another story of Nick Adams. Nick was nearly a man in this story, and he was on a solitary fishing trip deep in Michigan's woods. Hemingway worked at his desk at home, at tables in cafés, wherever he could find a place to concentrate deeply enough to bring Michigan to life. He was bringing Nick Adams to life as well, removing him from civilization, from the problems and anxieties of living among other people, isolating him— and through isolation allowing Nick to begin to come to terms with something, never mentioned in the story, which is troubling him.

"Inside the tent the light came through the brown canvas. It smelled pleasantly of canvas. Already there was something mysterious and homelike. Nick was happy as he crawled inside the tent. He had not been unhappy all day. This was different though. Now things were done. There had been this to do. Now it was done. He had made his camp. He was settled. Nothing could touch him. It was a good place to camp. He was there, in the good place. He was in his home where he had made it."

Nick had come to Michigan to fish the Two-Hearted River. At the rate of a few hundred words a day Hemingway brought the river to life, creating in almost every sentence the palpable presence of nature, of the ongoing struggle between life and death. When he finished the story Hemingway knew that he had written, in the oldest sense of the word, a masterpiece. "Big Two-Hearted River" proved to Hemingway that his apprenticeship was over.

His career as an editor neared its end as well. Ford Madox Ford had been displeased with the August *transatlantic review*: the issue held far too much American material. Ford had no time to assemble substitute stories and so had added a brief introduction in which he took Hemingway to task for his chauvinism. Embarrassed, Hemingway grew furious, and although he assisted on a few more issues his relationship with Ford was permanently damaged. When Ford printed another apology, this one for Hemingway's attack on T.S. Eliot, Hemingway quit the magazine and missed no opportunity publicly to insult and deride Ford.

Probably he would have left the magazine even without

Ford's annoyances. Hemingway had too many pressures upon his time. He was working on another long story, "The Undefeated," trying to bring what he knew of bullfights to fictional form. Bumby was growing, and Hemingway enjoyed spending afternoons with his son, strolling with him through the streets of Paris, a proud father showing off his boy. Boni and Liveright's interest in Hemingway had not abated, although Hemingway was also showing his short story collection to other publishers. He would stand more of a chance of securing a serious publisher, he knew, with the manuscript of a novel. He did not, however, feel he had sufficient control yet to undertake a book-length work, although he knew he would before long.

No matter how hard he was working, and no matter how many literary disputes he found himself involved in, Hemingway always made time for fun. As winter deepened in Paris, the Hemingways left for a long vacation in Austria. They traveled to Schruns, a skiing village where prices were sufficiently low to allow the poor family to live well. Hemingway and Hadley skied frequently, leaving happy Bumby in the good care of local girls whose health and strength impressed Hemingway. To celebrate the vacation he grew a full beard and did not cut his hair. The villagers applied a nickname of their own, referring to Hemingway as "the Black Christ."

Christmas, and then the New Year, passed without a book contract. Paris remained rainy and the Hemingways had not been home long before they returned to Schruns. In February 1925, Hemingway received a telegram that informed him that Boni and Liveright would publish his collection, which he called *In Our Time*. Its uppercase indicated the concessions he was willing to make to convention. His publishers soon asked for more.

While delighted with the quality of Hemingway's work, Boni and Liveright felt that some of the material was too strong for American tastes. Hemingway was dealing realistically in fiction with themes and incidents that were far more brutal and explicit than could be published. He was asked to delete part of "Mr. and Mrs. Elliot" and to remove entirely "Up in Michigan." American publishing and American readers were not yet ready for such honesty about the sexual act. Hemingway wrote another Nick Adams story to fill the hole in his book. This was a tale of Nick wandering like a hobo on the railroads, and of his encounter with a punch-drunk boxer. It was called "The Battler."

In Paris once more, Hemingway found that another publisher was eager to bring him into print. Charles Scribner's Sons was one of the most distinguished American publishing houses, and in 1925 its star writer was F. Scott Fitzgerald. Hemingway had become acquainted with Fitzgerald in Paris. Fitzgerald was prolific and successful, not only earning thousands of dollars apiece for short stories, but also—along with his wife Zelda—setting a style for the generation of young Americans now coming into their own. While Hemingway's most frequently visited literary territory was the Michigan woods, Fitzgerald's was the frantic world of the flapper, of speakeasy drinking and jazz dancing, of fraternity men and debutantes. Well dressed, spending freely, drinking heavily, Scott and Zelda Fitzgerald were as famous as movie stars, making news wherever they went, and 1925 was their season in Paris.

Hemingway and Hadley occasionally joined the Fitzgeralds for an evening, but Hemingway took part in the Fitzgeralds' revelry in much the same manner as he joined the bohemians. He watched, almost overtly studying his companions, frankly fascinated, and with almost equal frankness looking for material. The Fitzgeralds' life and pace was interesting, even exciting, but Hemingway thought that it was ultimately empty. He accompanied Scott Fitzgerald on an automobile trip, listening to his inebriated monologues, putting him to bed when he collapsed from drunkenness. Hemingway managed to be civil when the Fitzgeralds would appear, drunk, late at night, waking Bumby and Hadley. He felt that Fitzgerald was wasting his talent, corrupting it by grinding out stories tailored for high-paying markets rather than severely fashioned for their own artistic sake. When Fitzgerald asked Hemingway to read his new novel, *The Great Gatsby*, Hemingway recognized the book's greatness. *Gatsby*'s brilliance made Fitzgerald's dissipation of his gift seem even more pathetic to Hemingway.

Through Fitzgerald, Hemingway was introduced by mail to Maxwell Perkins, senior editor at Scribners. Perkins served as the guiding hand behind some of the most important literary careers of the day, and Hemingway's letter to him was courteous and polite. He explained to Perkins the nature of his contract with Boni and Liveright, which stipulated that Hemingway's next three books must be shown to that house first. Only if Boni and Liveright rejected a manuscript would Hemingway be free to show his work to another publisher.

Boni and Liveright's three-book option had been taken in expectation of a novel by Ernest Hemingway. A novel could find far greater success than a short story collection, and a book-length work was necessary to establish fully any writer's career. Hemingway began a novel, *Along with Youth*, which had Nick Adams as its protagonist. *Along with Youth* would deal with Nick's experiences in Italy during the First World War. Before he completed many pages, Hemingway realized that he would not finish the novel. It had no momentum; he could not make the story come alive. Perhaps Nick Adams was meant to be the focus only of short stories.

There was no reason his first novel must deal with the war. War was a large subject—the largest of subjects for writers, Hemingway often maintained—and he was not yet certain he had come to terms with it. The war would be there when he was ready to write about it, its horrors and excitements fixed in his memory to be brought to the page in the future.

For now the *effects* of World War I began to seem more likely subject matter for a novel. F. Scott Fitzgerald might have captured the frenetic pace of postwar American youth, but Hemingway had seen another face of war and its consequences.

He'd dealt with some of those consequences in his story of Krebs, "Soldier's Home," but that was a story in which the war was still a fresh experience. Now seven years had passed since the Armistice, but the bitterness, emptiness, and despair of the Americans and Europeans who had fought or lost loved ones to the fighting lingered. Gertrude Stein told Hemingway that all the youth who had gone to war, or sent lovers to the war, were displaced by the experience, that they were a lost generation. Hemingway began to think of that generation as the material from which a novel might be fashioned.

He would be traveling that summer with friends whose attitudes exemplified the aimlessness and loss of purpose of which Gertrude Stein had spoken. In the early summer of 1925, plans began to take shape for a trip to Spain, to the mountains for trout fishing and to Pamplona for the bullfights. Arrangements were made for Bumby to stay with friends. Harold Loeb, the Princeton graduate whose novel was to be published by Boni and Liveright, was among the gang bound for Spain, along with Bill Smith, Don Stewart, and Lady Duff Twysden. Thirty-two years old, separated from her husband and child, deeply cynical, Duff Twysden fascinated Hemingway. She was a bohemian who dressed in slacks and could hold her liquor as well as any man. Although involved in an affair with Loeb, she indulged in occasional romances with other men, and would not be bound by moral convention any more than by fashions in clothing. It was an interesting group; it would be an interesting trip.

The trout fishing in the Spanish mountains was a disappointment; the clear streams Hemingway recalled had been fouled by loggers and he caught no fish. He found Pamplona little better. The bullfights continued to work their spell over Hemingway, and he found himself especially interested in the performances of Cayetano Ordóñez, a nineteen-year-old prodigy of the bullring. Ordóñez accomplished miracles of great beauty with his cape and swords, captivating the Hemingways and delighting them when he dedicated a bull to Hadley and presented her with its ear. Despite the brilliance in the ring, the trip was spoiled for Hemingway by the crowds of wealthy Americans and English whose attraction to the bullfight was one of this year's fashion rather than dedication to a complex art. Hemingway was surrounded by phonies who understood nothing of the dignity of the bullfight, and certainly were not as mesmerized by it as was he.

There were tensions in Hemingway's group as well. Harold Loeb and Bill Smith were disgusted by the brutality of the bullfights; Duff Twysden spoke only of her fascination with the matadors' masculinity. Duff flirted openly with other men, causing Loeb embarrassment and sparking his anger. One morning she appeared with a black eye; she'd left Loeb the night before. One almost needed pencil and paper to keep track of who was speaking to whom. The group left Pamplona and traveled to Madrid, following Ordóñez, pressure among them building with every mile.

Hemingway released his own pressure in his art. He began a novel, one that soon established momentum. The novel, set in Spain, was about a matador who was obviously based on Ordóñez. Hemingway could not hold the focus of the novel upon the matador, however, and found his story proper in the events and relationships experienced by a group of expatriate Americans who had come to Spain to see the bullfights. He worked hard at the novel, trying alternate openings, sketching out scenes, building his cast of characters. The book would be narrated by Jake Barnes, an American journalist who during the war had been wounded in such a way as to render him incapable of sexual intercourse. Around Barnes, Hemingway assembled a group of characters that included Robert Cohn, a novelist, and Lady Brett Ashley, a cynical and promiscuous bohemian. In order to manage the conflicts and climax of the book—the trip to Spain—Hemingway had to establish his characters' background. He began the book again, this time in Paris.

"Robert Cohn was once middleweight boxing champion of

Princeton. Do not think that I am very much impressed by that as a boxing title, but it meant a lot to Cohn." With quick, deft passages Hemingway established Cohn's background, and made clear Cohn's fascination with Brett Ashley. "She stood holding the glass and I saw Robert Cohn looking at her. He looked a great deal as his compatriot must have looked when he saw the promised land. Cohn, of course, was much younger. But he had that look of eager, deserving expectation.

"Brett was damned good-looking. She wore a slipover jersey sweater and a tweed skirt, and her hair was brushed back like a boy's. She started all that. She was built with curves like the hull of a racing yacht, and you missed none of it with that wool jersey.

"'It's a fine crowd you're with, Brett,' I said."

Hemingway was working quickly now. He had found Jake Barnes's voice and he used it on page after page, writing in hotel rooms and restaurants, making clear Barnes's anguish over his wound, and Brett Ashley's own emotional agony over the futility of her feelings for Jake.

"The street was dark again and I kissed her. Our lips were tight together and then she turned away and pressed against the corner of the seat, as far away as she could get. Her head was down.

"'Don't touch me,' she said. 'Please don't touch me.'

"'What's the matter?'

"'I can't stand it.'

"'Oh, Brett.'

"'You mustn't. You must know. I can't stand it, that's all. Oh darling, please understand!' . . .

"'And there's not a damn thing we could do,' I said. . . .

"I lay awake thinking and my mind jumping around. Then I couldn't keep away from it, and I started to think about Brett and all the rest of it went away. I was thinking about Brett and my mind stopped jumping around and started to go in sort of smooth waves. Then all of a sudden I started to cry. . . .

"It is awfully easy to be hard-boiled about everything in the daytime, but at night it is another thing."

With Robert Cohn, Lady Brett Ashley, and others, Jake plans a trip to Pamplona for the fiesta. In company with an American, Bill Gorton, Jake stops first in the Spanish mountains to fish for trout. Robert Cohn's desperate romance with Brett Ashley is on his mind, but the fishing trip is the idyll at the center of the book, giving Jake the distance needed to rejoin Brett and Cohn. Hemingway had never written more beautifully of the tranquility to be found on a trout stream, of the companionship among fishermen, of the restorative powers of fishing, of the countryside. The fictional trout-fishing trip was far more successful than had been the real one Hemingway had taken just weeks before.

Too soon, though, and with a melancholy that becomes the reader's own, the idyll ends, and Jake and Bill travel to Pamplona to join the others for the fiesta. It is an ugly gathering. Brett torments Cohn with her affair with a matador, Pedro Romero. Jealousy and tension explode into violence, and shattered relationships. Characters' moral emptiness is revealed fully; revelry is used as a backdrop for the stripping of false fronts from personalities. Hemingway built the story to a high pitch, carrying it with him back to Paris, and finishing its first draft there, on September 21, 1925. After all the passion and pain, Jake and Brett share a final conversation.

"'You know I feel rather damned good, Jake.'

"'You should.'

"'You know it makes one feel rather good deciding not to be a bitch.'

"'Yes.' . . .

"A taxi came up the street, the waiter hanging out at the side. I tipped him and told the driver where to drive, and got in beside Brett. The driver started up the street. I settled back. Brett moved close to me. We sat close against each other. I put my arm around her and she rested against me comfortably. It was very hot and bright, and the houses looked sharply white. We turned out onto the Gran Via.

"'Oh, Jake,' Brett said, 'we could have had such a damned good time together.'

"Ahead was a mounted policeman in khaki directing traffic. He raised his baton. The car slowed suddenly pressing Brett against me.

"'Yes,' I said. 'Isn't it pretty to think so?'"

The first draft of the novel had taken him barely six weeks, and much of the book was written while traveling with people on whom Hemingway fashioned characters. More than once, a little drunk, he had bragged of how he was treating his frends in his novel, of how the book he was writing would show everyone what he really thought. Just as at the bullfights he insisted upon recognition as the only aficionado among the group, so did he now insist that his talent enabled him to use other people's lives as the foundation of a novel.

As fall neared he began preparing a final draft of the book, which as yet bore no title. During its construction he had thought of the book as *Fiesta*, but that was a Spanish word and he wanted something more easily recognized and understood by American audiences. *The Lost Generation*, Gertrude Stein's phrase, served as a working title for a while, but he ended by using it only as one of the book's epigraphs. After trying *River to the Sea, The Old Leaven*, and *Two Lie Together*, Hemingway selected his second epigraph, from Ecclesiastes; within it he found his book's title. "One generation passeth away," the passage from Ecclesiastes began, "and another generation cometh; but the earth abideth for ever. The sun also ariseth . . ." So, in the fall of 1925, Ernest Hemingway selected the title of his first novel: *The Sun Also Rises*.

With the season deepening, he was more concerned about the critical reaction to his first collection of short stories than his friends' reaction to their portraits in his novel. *In Our Time* was published by Boni and Liveright in October. The book received good reviews, with Hemingway being favorably compared to

Sherwood Anderson; his publishers had arranged for Anderson, their star writer, to provide a dust jacket quote endorsing Hemingway's work. All this was too much Anderson for Hemingway—he proclaimed loudly that he had long since surpassed Anderson as an artist. Proclamations notwithstanding, he had been helped by Anderson, he shared a publisher with Anderson, and he was compared to Anderson. By November, Hemingway had put aside his novel to work on a harsh parody of Anderson's most successful novel, *Dark Laughter.*

Hemingway called his parody *The Torrents of Spring.* He wrote it swiftly, in less than a month, lampooning Anderson's stylistic mannerisms and themes, using parody as a way of distancing himself from any accusation that he was Anderson's protégé. *The Torrents of Spring* upset Hadley, who valued Anderson's friendship, and infuriated Gertrude Stein. Hemingway ignored their objections and mailed the manuscript to Boni and Liveright. His publishers were expecting *The Sun Also Rises,* of which Hemingway had written them, not a novella that made cruel fun of one of their most profitable writers.

The Torrents of Spring was not the only source of discord between Hemingway and Hadley. Although they were happy during the completion of *The Sun Also Rises,* and at Hadley's thirty-fourth birthday—for which Hemingway borrowed money from a number of friends in order to purchase *The Farm,* a painting by Joan Miró—the couple were beginning to grow apart. Hemingway's fierce sense of competition seemed to create in him a determination to best every friend he had, whether with his fists, with quick and devastating insults, or in the pages of novels and satires. The poverty he and Hadley had shared, and in which they had discovered some genuine delight, no longer struck them as an adventure. It was, though not over, coming to an end. That Christmas, in Schruns, Hemingway bought Bumby a small rocking horse; Scott and Zelda Fitzgerald presented the toddler with a set of beautiful racing silks to wear as he rode.

Also in Schruns for the holidays was Pauline Pfeiffer, petite, chic, and with a bobbed haircut like a Fitzgerald heroine's. Pauline was no flighty flapper; she was on the Paris editorial staff of *Vogue* magazine. Pauline came from a wealthy Arkansas family, and was accustomed to a comfortable, privileged life-style. When, through mutual friends, she first met the Hemingways, she was disgusted with their poverty. It was not right to live that way, and there was no doubt in her mind that the couple was poor by choice. They could do much better if Ernest Hemingway were not so self-serving, so convinced of his artistic purpose. Pauline grew fond of Hadley, and as she spent more time with the family her opinion of Hemingway gradually changed. This was no poseur, she realized, and she realized as well that she had never met anyone like him. Over the course of Christmas 1925, her fascination deepened into a dangerous attraction.

In the midst of this difficult situation, there was news from America. A letter from his parents in Oak Park informed Hemingway of their disappointment in his work. They had read *In Our Time* and could find no good words for the brutality of vision expressed in Hemingway's stories. Dr. Hemingway promised that he and Grace would pray for their son. A telegram from Boni and Liveright was no more gratifying: they were rejecting *The Torrents of Spring*, but fully expected to publish *The Sun Also Rises*.

Hemingway knew better. By rejecting his parody, Boni and Liveright lost their claim on his novel. Hemingway wasted no time turning the rejection into an advantage, arranging for *The Torrents of Spring* to be submitted to Maxwell Perkins at Scribners. Interest was also expressed by the publishers Alfred Knopf and Harcourt, Brace, but Hemingway wanted Scribners to have first choice. He began to plan a trip to New York, during which he hoped to get his publishing affairs in order.

By late January 1926, he was ready to sail. He left Hadley and Bumby in Austria, then lingered in Paris for more than a week, spending his time with Pauline Pfeiffer and trying not to think of his wife and child, who waited patiently and hoped the trip was successful. Pauline offered, to Hemingway in person and to Hadley by letter, to accompany Hemingway to New York. Her letter pretended that the offer was innocent, but Hemingway and Pauline were already a topic of gossip.

She remained in Paris, however, and Hemingway spent most of February in New York. He met with Maxwell Perkins and was much impressed by the editor's intelligence and charm. He was even more impressed with the advance of $1,500 Perkins offered for *The Torrents of Spring* and *The Sun Also Rises*. In late February Hemingway returned to Europe, eager to share the good news with his family and let them know their hopes had been fulfilled. But when he reached Paris, Pauline was waiting for him, and their affair resumed. He delayed his departure for Schruns as long as he could. Arriving in Austria late and guilt-ridden, he found Hadley standing with Bumby in the train station, looking lovelier than anything he could imagine. Hemingway was filled with remorse and he spoke to his drinking companions of suicide. He thought that it would be better to be dead than to hurt Hadley.

They had been through so much together, so many false starts and disappointments. Now, with Scribners behind him, Hemingway knew that their dreams were beginning to be realized. But he also knew—already—that Hadley would not be sharing his triumph with him. The two tried hard in the spring of 1926 to hold their marriage intact, to recapture the magic that had illuminated their early days and nights in Paris. But Hemingway could not get Pauline out of his system, off his mind. In the spring Hadley confronted her husband with her knowledge of the affair. Hemingway grew furious, accusing Hadley of seeking to ruin their marriage by destroying his secrecy. It was all her fault, he said, and left for the Spanish bullfight season alone.

Hemingway spent three weeks in Spain, trying to sort out his thoughts, watching bullfights, writing short stories. He wrote again of Nick Adams in "Ten Indians" and "The Killers."

With his revision of *The Sun Also Rises* nearing completion, and *The Torrents of Spring* approaching publication, he made notes for a new novel. He chose *A New Slain Knight* as the book's tentative title, and plotted a story set in the United States, recounting the adventures and exploits of a criminal on the run. It would be a fine violent story, far different from *The Sun Also Rises*. Work, though, could not distract him from his family responsibilities, and in June he joined Hadley on the Riviera.

Hadley had arranged the loan of a villa in which to quarantine Bumby, who was suffering from whooping cough. The Fitzgeralds stayed nearby, and there were other friends close enough to visit. For a while it seemed that the Hemingways, with sickness focusing their attention, might survive as a family. That hope faded when Pauline Pfeiffer arrived at the villa, offering to help care for the child. Hadley said nothing. Pauline moved in, and later traveled with Hemingway and Hadley to Pamplona, following Bumby's recovery.

Back in Paris, the Hemingways arranged separate quarters. Hadley recognized that the marriage was over, asking only that Hemingway and Pauline spend one hundred days apart as a true test of their love. Pauline sailed for America. Hemingway embraced guilt with as much gusto as anything else in his life, stalking the streets of Paris, drinking hard, and telling everyone he encountered that he was the biggest son of a bitch in the history of the world. No one was more of a louse than Ernest M. Hemingway, he said, and if it weren't cowardly he would kill himself immediately rather than cause any more pain.

The Torrents of Spring was published to mixed, but generally unfavorable, reviews. However, anticipation of *The Sun Also Rises* began to build. Hemingway arranged for the novel to carry a dedication to Hadley and Bumby, and then signed over all the royalties to them. He cried as he helped Hadley settle into her new apartment. He spent a few days alone with Bumby, taking delight in his son, who spoke French and idolized his "Papa." In bars and at parties Hemingway insisted that everyone call him "Papa," and severed friendships brutally when he thought he detected a slight or a questioning of his judgment.

Published by Scribners in October 1926, *The Sun Also Rises* sold strongly, unusual for a first novel. It was well received critically, although the reaction from Oak Park was, as expected, less than enthusiastic. Although a trace of pride could be detected in Dr. Hemingway's letter to his son about the novel, Grace was openly disgusted that one of her offspring had written so filthy a book. Hemingway wrote an angry letter accusing his mother of disloyalty. He did not, however, inform his parents that he had left Hadley.

Pauline returned to France a week after the hundred days' separation expired. With winter nearing, Hemingway thought of skiing. This season he traveled, along with Pauline, to fashionable Gstaad, where they lived in company with the wealthy—a far cry from the happy peasants of Schruns, of whom Hemingway had grown so fond. His second novel, *A New Slain Knight*, had failed to come to life, and in Gstaad Hemingway began assembling the contents of a new collection of short stories for Scribners to publish in the fall of 1927. Hemingway called the book *Men Without Women* and worked on it between long days of skiing. In January 1927, when his divorce from Hadley became final, Hemingway was in Gstaad with Pauline.

By April plans were under way for a May wedding. There were certain religious technicalities to resolve, since Pauline was Roman Catholic. During the war, Hemingway claimed, he had been baptized a Catholic in a small Italian field hospital, and since his first marriage had taken place outside the Church he was able to renounce it as though it had never existed. The Church ruled his marriage to Hadley invalid, and gave permission for Hemingway and Pauline to be married. Bumby existed, though, wonderful proof of that first marriage, and Hemingway took every opportunity to have the child join him and Pauline as they traveled through Europe. His friends were disgusted at Hemingway's renunciation of his marriage to Hadley but he dismissed their criticisms with a firm look and the statement that he was Catholic now and because of that he must follow the laws of the Church.

As the wedding date neared, Hemingway became more than ever aware of the differences marriage to Pauline Pfeiffer would make in his life. Her relatives sent gifts of money, many of them checks for amounts nearly as large as the advance he'd received for *The Torrents of Spring* and *The Sun Also Rises*. Although he protested loudly that he would support his family with his writing, and while it was true that his short stories were beginning to earn larger sums, it was also clear that Pauline's money would make a dramatic change in the way Hemingway lived.

Ernest Hemingway and Pauline Pfeiffer were married on May 10, 1927. After a honeymoon of nearly a month, they hurried to Pamplona for the opening of the bullfight season. Hemingway's work that summer consisted primarily of preparing *Men Without Women* for publication. But he was also making notes for a second novel, this one a long and picaresque story of a rogue, not unlike *Tom Jones*. It was important, he felt, to do another novel soon and prove that *The Sun Also Rises*, which by now had sold more than 20,000 copies, was no fluke. By October, when *Men Without Women* was published, Hemingway had finished the early chapters of the novel. In America the public's reaction to the new collection was enthusiastic, and sales quickly exceeded 10,000 copies. The critics, though, were beginning to tire of Hemingway's unflinching realism and what they perceived as an adolescent's taste for the sordid. Some of their comments reminded Hemingway of his mother's opinion of his subject matter.

That fall he and Pauline learned that they would become parents the following year, and began to make plans for a return to the United States for the baby's birth. Pauline was frail and did not adjust well to her pregnancy, and both she and Hemingway felt it prudent to plan delivery in an American hospital.

Hemingway's own health became the object of some concern as in the space of a few weeks he was troubled by grippe, toothaches, and hemorrhoids. One night Bumby sleepily reached up to touch his father's face and by accident scratched Hemingway's good right eye, leaving him effectively blind for some time. He was in and out of bed all winter, feeling miserable, but forcing himself to make progress on the new novel. By the early months of 1928, as he and Pauline prepared to sail for America, Hemingway had nearly recovered from his various maladies. Then, in March, while reaching for the toilet chain in the middle of the night, Hemingway pulled by mistake the cord that opened the skylight. The window was old and cracked, and at Hemingway's tug it fell on his head, opening a long gash on his forehead. Pauline could not stop the bleeding and enlisted the poet Archibald MacLeish to help get Hemingway to a hospital. Nine stitches were required to close the cut, and the scar would be visible on Hemingway's forehead for the rest of his life. His vigorous pursuits had led to many accidents, with some calling Hemingway badly accident-prone, but this was his worst mishap since being wounded in Italy.

Italy was much on his mind as he prepared to leave for America, where he and Pauline would be staying in Piggott, Arkansas, her hometown. The picaresque novel had ground to a halt, but in spring 1928 Hemingway began to feel his novelistic confidence growing as it had not since the whirlwind first draft of *The Sun Also Rises*. He was twenty-eight years old and a decade had passed since the long night of his wounding. Perhaps in America he would be able to come to fictional terms with what was still the great experience of his life. He wrestled with an idea for a novel of the First World War.

In late March he and Pauline sailed for Havana. Their itinerary called for them to stay over in Key West, Florida, of which Hemingway had heard from John Dos Passos. Even before he saw it, the island fascinated Hemingway, and he and Pauline planned to stay there for several weeks. Pauline's doting and magnanimous uncle Gus Pfeiffer arranged to have a brand-new car in Key West for the couple when they arrived.

The voyage to Havana seemed to take forever. Pauline's discomfort grew worse. After more than two weeks at sea Havana was a relief, and the one-hundred-mile boat trip to Key West went by in an instant. The Florida island would be Hemingway's home for a while at least. He was eager to settle in and begin making real progress on his new novel. He had begun the book just a few weeks earlier, and already it looked as if it would be something special.

TEN

SUCCESS

KEY WEST, FLORIDA, in 1928 had a population of less than 10,000 scattered across its four-mile length. During the war there had been nearly three times that many people on the island, the growth a result of the booming navy yard there. Now the island, the southernmost city in the United States, had a sleepy tropical feel to it. Its tallest building was a seven-story hotel; most of the structures were considerably smaller, low houses, many of them with white surrounding walls, shaded by palms. Key West's hotels catered to tourists who were taken by the island's vaguely New England charm, its cupolas and porches—and, in contrast, the Bahamian settlers, known as "Conchs," whose accents, attitudes, and recipes contributed much to Key West's atmosphere.

Arriving near the end of the first week in April, Hemingway was immediately taken with the island's reality as he had been by others' recollections and descriptions of it. Uncle Gus Pfeiffer's car had not yet arrived, and the apologetic automobile dealer arranged for an apartment for the Hemingways. The apartment was small and hot, Pauline was miserable, but although railroad passage linked Key West to the mainland, Hemingway decided that they would stay on the island. He was already responding to it.

He soon established a routine that mixed creation with recreation. In the early mornings, when the apartment was still cool from the night breezes, he worked on his novel, writing in pencil for several hours. He broke off by early afternoon to walk the streets, getting to know the people, making himself known at the local bars. One spot in particular, a Conch bar called Sloppy Joe's after its owner, Joe Russell, became a favored spot. Above all, when he was not writing, Hemingway fished.

This was not the slow, graceful fly fishing he had loved since childhood. The waters around Key West, so near the Gulf Stream, were filled with strong fighting fish. Barracuda, permit, snapper, tarpon that weighed over one hundred pounds, and, farther out, sailfish and giant marlin—these were fish that challenged not only the fisherman's skills but also his endurance, determination, and sheer physical strength. This kind of fishing was a contest, even a battle, and it was precisely the sort of fishing Hemingway had been searching for. He got to know boat owners who ferried him to choice spots, learned the lore of ocean tackle and bait, and set himself the goal of becoming the finest sport fisherman the area had ever seen.

Hemingway seemed determined to fit into Key West and to accomplish his amalgamation quickly. He got rid of the necktie and jacket he'd worn during the voyage from Havana, and almost before his bags were unpacked had adopted a new uniform. Just as he'd strode through Paris in sweat shirt and tennis shoes, garb of the bohemian, he now dressed as a dockside tough, hard drinker, and hard fisherman—baggy trousers or shorts held up by a length of rope, torn shirt stained with the blood of fish, a shapeless billed cap pulled low over his eyes. He wore moccasins or went barefoot. His skin darkened quickly under the high sun and he stopped shaving. What he did in his apartment—writing—had nothing to do with the image he presented to Key West. He stood tall, his shoulders broad, with wide grin and knotted fists, someone ready at any time to rest himself against the pull of a tarpon, the punch of a brawler, the bite of rough liquor. People took to him and called him the "Old Master" as though he'd persuaded them to forget that he was still in his twenties.

When he could not get a boat he fished from the many docks around the port. He was standing there, line out, rod held high, on an afternoon a few days after his arrival, when he heard incredibly a bobwhite whistle. The whistle was an old signal between himself and his father. Hemingway looked up to see a passenger ship pulling into the docks, passengers lining the rails. He ran his eyes back and forth and was stunned to see his parents standing there, staring down at their son. Hemingway knew Dr. Hemingway and Grace were in Florida to visit property the doctor had purchased, and he had written asking them to visit, but he had not expected this. He dropped his fishing rod and ran for a gangplank reunion.

If Dr. and Mrs. Hemingway were startled by their son's bearded, grimy appearance, Hemingway was shaken by his father's looks. All of the vigor had gone out of Clarence Hemingway. He looked old; his clothes were baggy, his hair white. In the years since Hemingway had last seen his father, the doctor had developed diabetes and a heart condition. His grip held only a hint of the strength he'd once possessed. Grace was still strong, though, larger than ever and just as cautious in giving her approval to her son. The family spent an afternoon together, and despite their disappointment at Hemingway's divorce— both Dr. and Mrs. Hemingway remained devoted to Hadley— they were cordial to Pauline. When they parted Hemingway expressed his hope that his father's health would soon improve. Left unspoken was Grace's hope that her son would see the light and begin writing more inspirational works.

Hemingway at least was inspired by his work. He could not wait to get to it each morning, and even the banging of mechanics at the garage beneath their apartment could not distract him from the story he was telling. He was determined to put everything he had into this novel, to create a masterpiece. All of the lessons he'd learned during his apprenticeship, everything he believed about prose and narrative, were bent to the task of bringing his wartime experiences to life.

He began by fixing time and place as carefully as he ever did. "In the late summer of that year we lived in a house in a village that looked across the river and the plain to the mountains. In the bed of the river there were pebbles and boulders, dry and white in the sun, and the water was clear and swiftly moving and blue in the channels. Troops went by the house and down the road and the dust they raised powdered the leaves of the trees. The trunks of the trees too were dusty and the leaves fell early that year and we saw the troops marching along the road and the dust rising and leaves, stirred by the breeze, falling and the soldiers marching and afterward the road bare and white except for the leaves." Hemingway was in Key West but when he held his pencil he was in Italy and eighteen once more.

His narrator, Frederic Henry, a young American ambulance driver on the Italian front, a volunteer, becomes involved with an English nurse, Catherine Barkley. It is for Henry at first a flirtation, "a game, like bridge, in which you said things instead of playing cards." Cynical and at the same time a romantic, Henry is fascinated by Catherine Barkley, who, because of grief over a lost love, seems at times to have only the slightest of grips on her sanity.

By the book's ninth chapter Hemingway had established his characters, and it was time to elevate the novel's stakes. Frederic Henry is at the front, eating with his Italian friends. "I ate the end of my piece of cheese and took a swallow of wine. Through the other noise I heard a cough, then came the chuh-chuh-chuh-chuh—then there was a flash, as when a blast-furnace door is swung open, and a roar that started white and went red and on and on in a rushing wind. I tried to breathe but my breath would not come and I felt myself rush bodily out of myself and out and out and out and all the time bodily in the wind. I went out swiftly, all of myself, and I knew I was dead and that it had all been a mistake to think you just died. Then I floated, and instead of going on I felt myself slide back. I breathed and I was back. The ground was torn up and in front of my head there was a splintered beam of wood. In the jolt of my head I heard somebody crying. I thought somebody was screaming. I tried to move but I could not move."

In the Milan hospital to which he is transferred for the treatment of his severe leg wounds, Frederic Henry's flirtation with Catherine Barkley deepens, grows deeply physical and passionate. Before returning to the front Henry learns that Catherine is pregnant. He reaches the front in time for the Italians' disastrous, chaotic retreat from Caporetto. At his desk each morning, his memory of the war mingling with his recollection of the Greeks' flight from Constantinople, all made larger by his imagination, Hemingway captured the terror, the rain and the mud, the shrieks of the wounded, summary executions, the sense of despair that filled the retreating troops and the civilians who with their pitiful belongings fled alongside them. He inserted no romance about the magnificence of war, using magnificent prose only to capture its reality, as he had seen it, to make it real for his readers. He was twenty-eight years old and in absolute control of his material.

Away from the desk he tried not to think about the book. He had no title for it yet. The groundwork had been laid for a tragic, moving climax following Henry's desertion from the retreat, but it would not be easy to achieve that tragedy on the page. When Waldo Pierce, a painter he'd known in Paris, and John Dos Passos appeared in Key West, Hemingway had to work hard not to talk about the book. It seemed so good that it frightened him, and at the same time he was genuinely frightened that he might be deluding himself. He was too close to the book: how could he know whether or not it was any good? The best thing to do was to leave the novel on his desk when he quit work each day, to try to forget it, and to seek with his friends distractions from literature.

They were not hard to find. Hemingway had assembled a crew again, the "Mob," as he called them: Dos Passos, Pierce, bar owner "Josie" Russell, charter boat captain Eddie ("Bra")

Saunders. He grew especially close to Charles Thompson, a wealthy Key West businessman whose interest in sport fishing was as deep as Hemingway's. The Mob drank and fished together nearly every afternoon, Hemingway trying to best all of them with the largest fish landed, the most liquor drunk, the best exhibitions of strength, endurance, and masculinity. It was all a contest. Through Charles Thompson's influence they were permitted to use the swimming facilities at the navy yard, and there staged elaborate high-diving contests. Hemingway's effort was labeled by the others the "Hemingswan," an inadvertent combination of the swan dive and the belly flop; he was not amused. One day, after nearly two hours' struggle with a 138-pound tarpon, Waldo Pierce dove into the water to wrestle the six-foot fish ashore barehanded. Even Hemingway was impressed. Together the Mob raided bookstores, held eating competitions in restaurants, sang bawdy songs, made fun of each other, and had fun together. By late spring they were being taken on charter boats to remote spots for overnight fishing expeditions.

As June neared it was time for Hemingway and Pauline to be on their way to Piggott for the birth of their child. Pauline left early by train, leaving Hemingway to drive the new Ford, which had finally arrived. He had company on the drive, for Pauline's father had come to Key West to meet his new son-in-law. Hemingway, unwilling to alter his behavior in the least to impress Pauline's father, immediately made Paul Pfeiffer a member of the Mob. If he was startled at first by Hemingway's appearance, Pfeiffer also noted that Hemingway left the Mob early each evening to retire for a good night's sleep before resuming work on his novel at dawn the next day. It was an impressive display of discipline. By the time of their long drive together, by ferry through those Keys without highway links, and then more than a thousand miles across country, the two had established good relations.

Piggott, Arkansas, was a solid, conservative small town and

seemed after Key West excruciatingly dull to Hemingway. He got on well with Pauline's family, especially her mother and Uncle Gus, but good relations and family were no substitute for excitement. He talked of taking Pauline to the Michigan woods; she could have her baby in Petoskey, and he would be close to good fishing with his father. Dr. Hemingway, however, advised against that idea—the Petoskey hospital was unsuitable for what was likely to be a difficult delivery. Hemingway and Pauline finally went to Kansas City, Missouri. After more than a day's labor, their son Patrick was delivered by Caesarean section on June 28, 1928. The baby weighed nine and a half pounds, and his birth left Pauline weak and ill.

Hemingway stayed close by for a month, continuing to work on his novel, which was now nearly five hundred pages long. As Pauline recovered, Hemingway's restlessness grew unbearable. It was July, the fishing was wonderful in Key West, the bulls were running in Pamplona, and he was stuck in the Midwest with a frail wife and a child who was, of course, wonderful but no company at all. Late in July he packed his manuscript, called a friend, and drove to Wyoming for some serious trout fishing. He lingered a few days at a dude ranch, but there was too much dude and not enough ranch—he wanted to get away from civilization. Driving alone, he pushed deeper and deeper into the West, his progress shadowed by the imposing presence of the Bighorn Mountains.

In early August, her strength recovered, Pauline brought Patrick to join Hemingway at a ranch in Sheridan, Wyoming. Hemingway took his fly rod out each afternoon to measure himself against the big Western trout, but his manuscript held most of his attention. Some days he wrote nearly ten pages, a phenomenal rate of production for him. He knew how the book would end now: he could feel it and see it, and he knew that he could write it. Pauline's difficulties during the delivery were fresh in his mind as he brought Catherine Barkley into the labor neither she nor her child would survive. Now was the time to take each day's work slowly, to get every word right, to fight the impulse to race through to the end of the book. Hemingway took most of August to finish the first draft of the novel, and when it was done he was as profoundly exhausted as he had ever been.

His antidote, as always, was action. Hemingway prescribed for himself a discipline of calisthenics, roadwork and shadowboxing, long tramps to fish or hunt. He put the novel, still untitled, out of his mind. There was another draft to do but he could not hurry it. He wanted to settle down first, lose weight, get himself back into shape, take stock, and make plans. He'd turned twenty-nine during the summer of Patrick's birth, and it was time to begin thinking of a home.

As far as Hemingway was concerned, there was only one location for that home: Key West. He could not get the island out of his mind. He could write there—he had proved that already—and he could fish and have fun there. Home for him meant a base of operations, and there was no better base than Key West, Florida. Pauline had developed a close friendship with Charles Thompson's wife, Lorine, and wrote her now to begin looking for a house suitable for the Hemingways.

Men Without Women had now sold nearly 20,000 copies, but most of the royalties went to Hadley. The new novel would be the first book from which Hemingway himself earned much money, and the money quickly became impressive. Less than two months after the completion of the first draft, and without seeing any of the book, Maxwell Perkins wrote to guarantee serialization in *Scribner's Magazine.* His letter included an offer of $10,000 for the serial rights. Hemingway was excited but cautious. He wanted to put his house in order first, to establish residence in Key West and get on with the revision. He was actively searching for titles in the Bible, in Shakespeare, in books of poetry. He would wait until the book was completed before accepting. During November he traveled to New York to discuss the book with Perkins, made arrangements for his sister Sunny to come to Key West to help with the typing of the novel, and paid a call in Oak Park, where he was disappointed to find that his father's health and demeanor had worsened. The doctor could not get his mind off his financial situation, which involved large investments in Florida real estate and equally burdensome family debts that were coming due. Hemingway offered what encouragement he could. Late in the month he drove Pauline and Patrick to Key West, where they settled into a spacious rented house. Hemingway did not stay there long. Bumby was to spend Christmas with his father, who would return the boy to Paris in the spring. Hadley had placed the five-year-old boy in the care of stewards and stewardesses for his first solo Atlantic crossing. Hemingway left Florida almost immediately for New York to meet his son.

He traveled by train and used part of the time to write a letter to his father. Hemingway told the doctor not to worry about his debts. A large advance was coming; he would be able to help his father. Hemingway mailed the letter during a stop in Jacksonville, and passed the rest of the trip in anticipation of again seeing Bumby, his fine son who was so sophisticated he looked like a seasoned world traveler as he descended the gangplank in New York to hug his Papa. It was a happy reunion, and they spent nearly all of Hemingway's pocket money on Christmas presents before boarding a Key West–bound train on December 6, 1928.

A telegram from his sister Carol was waiting for Hemingway in the Trenton, New Jersey, train station. His father had died that morning. Hemingway contacted Maxwell Perkins and asked him to send $100 by wire to Philadelphia, the next stop. The money had not come when the train arrived, and Hemingway dispatched hurried telegrams for assistance to both Waldo Pierce and Scott Fitzgerald. Fitzgerald responded immediately, wiring the asked-for sum to Hemingway at the station. Hemingway tipped a porter to care for Bumby on the journey south, while he caught the next train to Oak Park.

It was only after he arrived in Illinois that Hemingway

learned the details of his father's death. Depressed over his health as much as his finances, unable because of his diabetes to eat the foods he most enjoyed, seeing no prospect for an improvement in the condition of his life, Dr. Hemingway had that morning placed the barrel of a .32 caliber Smith and Wesson pistol behind his right ear and killed himself. Hemingway dealt with the funeral and made what plans he could for the disposition of the estate, asking for himself only the pistol with which his father had committed suicide. In private he blamed the tragedy on his mother's demands, her expensive social ambitions, as much as on his father's failing health, but publicly promised to help Grace as much as he was able. Drained emotionally and physically, he finally returned to Key West and the revision of the novel.

Throughout the fall of 1928, he had tried and rejected titles for the book. At last, thumbing through the *Oxford Book of English Verse,* he came across the work of George Peele and from that sixteenth-century poet took his title. He would call the book *A Farewell to Arms.* With Hemingway putting in long days, at the end of which he gave Sunny a handful of pages for final typing, the revision of the novel took little more than a month. Maxwell Perkins came down from New York to read the manuscript, but Hemingway seemed more interested in introducing the staid New England editor to the joys of sport fishing and heavy drinking. They spent nearly a week in each other's company, getting to know each other well for the first time. The novel was even more impressive than Perkins had imagined, and he bought its serial rights for *Scribner's Magazine* for $16,000, a record sum. Hemingway arranged to send monthly payments to his mother to help with her finances, although he continued to denounce her at every opportunity. In return, she shipped him the pistol Dr. Hemingway had used to take his life. Hemingway told Sunny that suicide wasn't so bad, and that it was probably the way he would himself die.

By April 1929, Hemingway, Pauline, Patrick, and Bumby,

with Sunny in tow, set sail for Paris. *A Farewell to Arms* was about to appear as a serial and Hemingway's nerves were stretched tight. The ending on which he had worked so hard no longer pleased him, and he revised it virtually until publication day. Seeking an outlet for his energy, he began boxing once more, setting up a match with a Toronto friend, Morley Callaghan, with Scott Fitzgerald serving as timekeeper. Fitzgerald, who had responded so promptly to Hemingway's need for traveling money, had lately found himself in career doldrums. *The Great Gatsby* had not been the overwhelming success he'd hoped for, and his and Zelda's high life was bringing them close to the edge of financial ruin. Shaky and uncertain, his admiration for Hemingway remained constant. He was so impressed with Hemingway's physical size and strength that, during the match with Callaghan, he concentrated more on the boxing than on the time. The one-minute round stretched out to four minutes, with Hemingway getting into deeper and deeper trouble. Finally Callaghan knocked Hemingway down, and only then did Fitzgerald realize his mistake. It was an accident, but Hemingway cursed furiously, glaring at Fitzgerald.

In the summer Hemingway took Pauline to Spain for the bullfight season, hoping to recapture some of the excitement he had found there earlier. Instead he found large crowds of Americans, a tourist invasion that might in part have been prompted by *The Sun Also Rises* and its portrait of *fiesta.* The only positive aspect of this American influx that Hemingway found was an American matador who called himself Sidney Franklin. Franklin, whose real name was Frumpkin and who had been reared in Brooklyn, was the rage of the season, a true master of the bullring. Hemingway followed Franklin from stadium to stadium for weeks, beginning to think that he might write a book about the bullfight. Perhaps it would be wise to follow the novel with a work of nonfiction.

Bearing a dedication to Gus Pfeiffer, *A Farewell to Arms* was published in September 1929, and in less than a month had sold nearly 30,000 copies. Hemingway was the most widely discussed writer in America, and not even the collapse of the stock market on October 29 could slow his sales. At thirty there was no doubt of his success. Every best-seller list in the country showed Hemingway's name at the top. Magazines tracked him down, cabling offers of thousands of dollars for a few thousand words. Theatrical producers and motion picture companies expressed interest in the new novel as the basis for dramatic works, and in Hemingway as a screenwriter. He had no desire to write for the movies, no matter how regal the salary offered. He was, he said, one novelist and short story writer who would remain true to himself and his artistic integrity.

He was not doing a great deal of writing, however. He and Pauline remained in Europe well into 1930, returning to Key West in February. They rented another home while continuing to look for a piece of property to purchase. Hemingway could not get started on another book, although he was collecting material and photographs about the bullfight, and produced an article on the subject for *Fortune* magazine.

With *A Farewell to Arms* doing so well, Hemingway did not let his lack of production get him down. There were too many things to do, most importantly the assembly of another Mob with which to make an ambitious assault upon the area's fish. He persuaded Max Perkins to come down from New York and join a group on a trip to the Dry Tortugas, where the fishing was unbelievable and there were neither women nor the worries of work. A heavy storm stranded them on an island for more than two weeks; even Perkins grew a beard and stopped bathing. They ran out of staples, including liquor, and their diet consisted for a time solely of fish. Hemingway stood on the beach, staring at the enormous waves as though defying them to take him on. He was more than their match and more than a match for any fish that swam beneath them. The stranding was no hardship, but a wonderful, manly adventure, the sort of thing pirates had faced in the books he'd read as a youth. When the storm broke and the group returned to Key West, it was with the melancholy sense of the end of something special.

The adventure had rejuvenated Hemingway's creative energies, and by the summer of 1930 he was ready to begin his bullfight book. This, he maintained, would be the largest challenge he'd yet faced as a writer. He wanted to make an unfamiliar and symbolic sport accessible to American readers, and at the same time establish himself and his credentials as an *aficionado*, while capturing with his prose the spirit and flavor of the Spain he loved so deeply. The book would have a large section of photographs, which Hemingway would select, and a glossary that he would compile himself. He set to work in early summer.

"At the first bullfight I ever went to I expected to be horrified and perhaps sickened by what I had been told would happen to the horses. Everything I had read about the bull ring insisted on that point; most people who wrote of it condemned bullfighting outright as a stupid brutal business, but even those that spoke well of it as an exhibition of skill and as a spectacle deplored the use of horses and were apologetic about the whole thing. The killing of the horses in the ring was considered indefensible. I suppose, from a modern moral point of view, that is, a Christian point of view, the whole bullfight is indefensible; there is certainly much cruelty, there is always danger, either sought or unlooked for, and there is always death, and I should not try to defend it now, only to tell honestly the things I have found true about it. To do this I must be altogether frank, or try to be, and if those who read this decide with disgust that it is written by someone who lacks their, the readers', fineness of feeling I can only plead that this may be true. But whoever reads this can only truly make such a judgment when he, or she, has seen the things that are spoken of and knows truly what their reactions to them would be."

The first paragraph and the early chapters set the tone for the book, serving to establish a credo as well as introduce a subject. Hemingway made his authority and expertise clear—he would not write of anything he had not seen firsthand and did not know absolutely to be true. It was also clear that he felt free to vary his pace, to take digressions. He spoke openly of himself and of the days when he saw his first bullfights, when he was learning to write; his tone was now that of a master looking back upon his apprenticeship. He introduced the technical details of the bullfight lucidly, his material well organized and his prose clear and understandable. For long passages the book became a travelogue with Ernest Hemingway as a guide to the sights, sounds, smells, and tastes of Spain. Not quite a quarter of the way through the book he introduced another voice, the "Old Lady," who asked questions, made comments, and led Hemingway into areas that seemed far removed from Spain and matadors.

"*Old Lady:* Then I may take it that you have abandoned the bull ring even as an amateur?

"Madame, no decision is irrevocable, but as age comes on I feel I must devote myself more and more to the practice of letters. My operatives tell me that through the fine work of Mr. William Faulkner publishers now will publish anything rather than try to get you to delete the better portions of your works, and I look forward to writing of those days of my youth which were spent in the finest whorehouses in the land amid the most brilliant society there found. I had been saving this background to write of in my old age when with the aid of distance I could examine it most clearly.

"*Old Lady:* Has this Mr. Faulkner written of these places?

"Splendidly, Madame. Mr. Faulkner writes admirably of them. He writes the best of them of any writer I have read for many years.

"*Old Lady:* I must buy his works.

"Madame, you can't go wrong on Faulkner. He's prolific too. By the time you get them ordered there'll be new ones out."

Hemingway had found a form for nonfiction that delighted

him. He could do anything in this book without losing its focus. That focus, finally, was the same as the bullfight's: it was a book about death. He selected *Death in the Afternoon* as his title and carried the manuscript with him when he took Pauline and Bumby to the Nordquist ranch in Wyoming, near Montana, for a summer of hunting and fishing. He wanted to try himself against large Western game.

The opportunity for the test soon arose. A bear had been killing local cattle and Hemingway was eager to bring it down. Along with Lawrence Nordquist, owner of the ranch, he rode high into the hills, where they killed a horse and then built a fire upon the carcass in order to raise a smell that would attract the bear. When they returned a few days later, the huge brown bear stood in clear sight, feasting upon the dead horse. Hemingway took careful aim and killed the bear with a single shot. A week later he took Bumby up to see the bear bait, and the boy, now six, saw his first elk, and then watched as his father killed another bear, this one a black, again with a single shot. Hemingway added to the tally during the following weeks, catching dozens of trout, killing mountain ram and elk. Key West had brought him the fishing for which he'd searched; now he was discovering big game hunting.

He tried each morning to get in some work on *Death in the Afternoon,* but more often than not he allowed himself to be talked into fishing or hunting. The book could wait: Dos Passos was joining him soon and together they would explore the beautiful Western hills. With Dos Passos he took a long automobile trip to Yellowstone, and was driving them back to the Nordquists' at night when Hemingway was blinded by the lights of another car. He pulled sharply to the right to avoid a collision and his car flipped into a deep ditch beside the road. Dos Passos was only shaken, but Hemingway was pinned for some time behind the wheel of the car. When he was finally extricated, it was obvious that his right arm was badly broken. Dos Passos flagged down a car to take them to the nearest hospital. To keep

the broken bone from grating, Hemingway placed his arm between his knees and pressed them tight together. The ride took
most of an hour.

The fracture was even worse than they'd suspected. An
operation was required, during which the arm was opened and
the ends of the bone tied together. Hemingway, remembering
perhaps his father's advice about pain, refused to complain. Pain
did not bother him; he had known pain before. He amused
himself by making a catalogue of the injuries he'd suffered and
the number of stitches he'd taken since signing his first contract
with Scribners. What did concern Hemingway was the loss, if
only for a time, of his writing hand. It would mean the postpone-
ment of *Death in the Afternoon,* which he'd hoped to complete
before the beginning of 1931. With his arm in a sling there was
no way he could write. Hemingway was by temperament incapable of dictating worthwhile prose and he resigned himself to
the month's bed rest insisted upon by his doctor. The daily mail,
newspapers, and a small radio were his only distractions.

He remained in the hospital in Billings, Montana, until
nearly Christmas, and his mood blackened each day. Friends
who traveled cross-country to wish him well were greeted with
curses and suspicion: hadn't they come to pay their last respects? He refused to have his beard trimmed or his hair cut. By
the time he was released he looked something like Rasputin:
thick black hair and beard surrounding penetrating eyes. As
though deliberately to annoy Pauline, he continued to boycott
the barber and paraded around Piggott in cowboy clothes. He
took delight in his defiant posture until a group of schoolchil-
dren, assuming he was a hobo, chased him down the street,
tossing snowballs at him and attempting to run him out of town.
He soon shaved and cleaned himself.

Postures of defiance or superiority were beginning to seem
more and more natural to Hemingway. He felt he had good
reason for his cockiness. He was stronger than anyone he met,
taller, able to drink more, a better writer. He was also lately

more successful: the motion picture rights to *A Farewell to Arms*—its title almost ironic, as his own right arm hung in a sling—brought him almost $25,000. *Death in the Afternoon,* he felt certain, would serve as the capstone on his ascent, establishing him as a man of letters, a master of nonfiction as well as of the novel and the short story. When Sinclair Lewis won the Nobel Prize for Literature in 1930, he mentioned Hemingway in his acceptance speech. Hemingway was angered that Lewis also mentioned Thomas Wolfe. As far as Ernest Hemingway was concerned, he had no real competition as champion of American literature, and he intended to use the thirties, both the nation's and his own, to prove it.

ELEVEN

SPORTSMAN

HIS FRACTURED ARM KEPT Hemingway from his desk until nearly spring. He dictated occasional correspondence to Pauline, much of it reading like situation reports on the state of his health and his continuing literary reputation. As the New Year began, he taught himself to slowly scratch left-handed with a pencil. He could work a typewriter at the rate of three or four words a minute. There was, he maintained, no point in even thinking about serious writing. How could wonderful prose be dictated? How could you follow the dialogue when it came fast, as it sometimes did? Narrative had to be worked carefully, with the point of a pencil. When dialogue began to flow and characters at last began truly to speak, the typewriter was perfect. The only thing his left hand was good for was holding a shotgun poorly: his chest grew black and blue from the kick and slip of the gun.

At least he was getting some shooting in. He was planning a lot more. As his fascination with hunting deepened, he began to develop a theory of the sport, a code stating that it must be done properly in order to have any meaning. Hunting was a test of many things: endurance, stealth, steadiness of nerves, sharpness of sight. Against the largest game, it could be quite dangerous, and so it was a test of courage. No hunter could really know how good he was, Hemingway came to believe, until he had measured himself against the largest game in the world. He was thinking seriously of a hunting trip to Africa. When he mentioned the idea casually to Gus Pfeiffer, Pauline's uncle on the spot offered to finance the trip, and put no ceiling on the budget. Hemingway could do it as it should be done, in fine and expensive style. Some plans had been made for a safari in the spring of 1931, a reward to follow the completion and publication of *Death in the Afternoon*. The broken arm changed all that. Hemingway subscribed to hunting journals and ordered books on Africa. If he must wait, he could at least use the time to enlarge his knowledge and theories of the art and sport of big game hunting.

By March his hand was strong enough for at least a smaller adventure. Max Perkins was coming to Key West once more. A new gang was assembled and the Tortugas freshly assaulted. This season did not equal the previous one, already becoming a legend. Again a storm pinned Hemingway to a remote island, but only after Perkins had returned to New York. His companions now did not delight Hemingway and he began pointing out to them the ways in which they failed to meet his standards. When a broken engine left them unable to replenish their ice for more than a week, Hemingway exploded. Hundreds of pounds of fish—his whole huge catch—spoiled, and Hemingway prodded and berated the others to the edge of violence. He could handle that, too, he made clear, but when challenged his anger turned instantly to charm, his scowl to a grin as wide as the sky. He had a lot on his mind, he explained; Papa, as he called himself, was just edgy.

Pauline's thoughts were concerned for a time with making a permanent home in Key West. Gus Pfeiffer, feeling it was time for the couple to own a piece of property, provided the down payment for a large house at 907 Whitehead Street. The house was so run-down that neighborhood children claimed it was haunted. Whether or not there were any ghosts, an extensive and expensive renovation lay ahead. The roof, wiring, plumbing, plaster, and floors had to be replaced before the house was ready for occupancy. The house was purchased in April but the work, it turned out, would have to wait until fall. By May Hemingway was feeling ready to write again, to get himself back into shape for the completion of *Death in the Afternoon*. He had been away from the book for months; in order to restore its tone and feel, Hemingway felt the need first to visit his source— Spain!

This season he ignored the tourists and concentrated on the mood of the Spanish people. Political tension in the country was thick. King Alfonso XIII had gone into exile, his monarchy replaced by a nominally democratic government. But it was a weak government beset by pressures from many sides: the military, the Catholic Church, fascists, socialists, left- and right-wing groups. Hemingway heard the word *revolution* mentioned more than once. Ever since he was a young reporter, he'd bragged of his acute political sense; now he sensed no easy way for Spain out of her troubles. Sooner or later the tension would erupt and the results would be tragic. For now he listened to gossip, collected photographs, made notes on the current bullfight season for his final draft, and selected terms and wrote definitive essays for *Death in the Afternoon*'s glossary. By September Pauline was well into her second pregnancy and they were readying themselves for the return to America and the child's birth.

Hemingway hoped for a daughter, but on November 12, 1931, a son, Gregory, was born in Kansas City. Before Christmas the family returned to Key West, where work on the house on Whitehead Street was well begun. Although the main house was in considerable disrepair, the workers were instructed to turn their attention first to the small building that had served as a carriage house with servants' quarters on the second floor. The carriage house was to be Hemingway's workroom, detached from household noises and disturbances, and when repairs were complete he installed himself and his notes in it. He hurried to his office at first light each morning, and began working over the last draft of *Death in the Afternoon*.

The main house was chaotic through the holidays. Pauline's

second Caesarean had left her drained and weak; the children's cribs required cheesecloth draped over them to catch falling plaster; Patrick sprayed the new baby with insecticide and shortly thereafter ate ant poison. The children recovered, the renovation proceeded, and Hemingway brought a Christmas tree to Pauline's bedroom, where she was confined for rest. Increasingly, though, he sought the privacy of his office, moving almost without pause from the completion of *Death in the Afternoon* to the creation of a new book.

A Farewell to Arms had consolidated Hemingway's position as a novelist, just as he was convinced *Death in the Afternoon* would establish his preeminence as a man of letters. Now it was time to return to the form that had brought him his first fame: he began writing short stories once more. He had never completely abandoned the form, but the early months of 1932 found him writing story after story, a rate of productivity unusual for Hemingway. He called such times *belles epoques*, beautiful periods when, in literature at least, he could do no wrong. He incorporated material from Key West in stories such as "After the Storm," and also recalled his days in Kansas City as a cub reporter for "God Rest You Merry, Gentlemen." "A Way You'll Never Be" was another story of Nick Adams's experiences in the war. Before summer he had assembled much of the contents of a new short story collection.

The depression deepened during the early 1930s, and Gus Pfeiffer, though hardly ruined, found cash tight and informed Hemingway that his offer of financing for a safari would have to be postponed until the economy improved. Hemingway was impatient to go after the large African game, but sought to cushion his disappointment by pursuing marlin, the largest sport fish in the sea. He made himself virtually an apprentice to Carlos Gutiérrez, a Cuban in his sixties who had fished for marlin for nearly half a century. Marlin grew to more than one thousand pounds, and their graceful leaps, the valiance with which they strained against the line, the fight they waged until their hearts gave out, their beauty and their strength all combined to make them the sport fish Hemingway had sought all his life. He caught nearly two dozen in his first weeks of fishing for them.

With Africa unavailable for this year at least, Hemingway and Pauline returned to the Nordquists' ranch in Wyoming, leaving the children in Piggott, Arkansas. The West was as beautiful as Hemingway recalled (he had captured some of its beauty in a story called "Wine of Wyoming") and now he rode almost daily through the hills in search of trout or game. He tried each morning to put in a few hours at a desk, correcting proof for *Death in the Afternoon*, or working on *Winner Take Nothing*, his new short story collection. He wrote, rode, and hunted throughout the late summer, measuring his kills against others', insistent that he be acknowledged the best, steadiest shot.

Hemingway enjoyed hunting bear, but by fall he was ready to arm himself for an expedition in search of more ferocious quarry: critics. *Death in the Afternoon* had been published by Scribners and the reviews were worse than unfavorable. Virtually every newspaper and magazine found fault with the book, with complaints ranging from the usual disapproval of Hemingway's use of coarse language, to concern about too deep a fascination with death. More than one reviewer felt that Hemingway's assertions of masculinity were becoming overblown and melodramatic, the posture of an adolescent, not a man of literature. Hemingway vented part of his anger by making a Christmas duck-hunting trip to Piggott, for which he ordered more than two thousand shotgun shells.

The *belle epoque* extended itself into 1933, with more short stories taking shape. "The Gambler, the Nun, and the Radio" was based upon the month spent in a Montana hospital bed. He attempted in a story called "Homage to Switzerland" to come to fictional terms with the pain he still felt over leaving Hadley. Each of the stories in *Winner Take Nothing* approached the subject of courage; each dealt in some way with death or loss. Hemingway continued to refine his craft, using it to explore his vision of the world, his understanding of what one could expect from life. The title of the collection was itself one enunciation of his vision.

Another was the story "A Clean, Well-Lighted Place," in which Hemingway used the thoughts of an old waiter to state clearly his belief that nothing—*nada*, in Spanish—was all anyone could expect. "What did he fear? It was not fear or dread. It was nothing that he knew too well. It was all a nothing and a man was a nothing too. It was only that and light was all it needed and a certain cleanliness and order. Some lived in it and never felt it but he knew it all was nada y pues nada y nada y pues nada. Our nada who art in nada, nada be thy name thy kingdom nada thy will be nada in nada as it is in nada. Give us this nada our daily nada and nada us our nada as we nada our nadas and nada us not into nada but deliver us from nada; pues nada. Hail nothing full of nothing, nothing is with thee." The story was bitter and it was melodramatic, but it also stated Hemingway's position and it was clear. Winner or loser—it made no difference; nothingness was all that waited.

One consequence of Hemingway's philosophy was an increasing disinterest in politics. People were out of work all around him, the economy was shattered. Writers were bending their talents to the task of rebuilding the world, and using their talents to make that reconstruction revolutionary. Politics in the modern world, they argued, was the most important subject for a writer; anything else was self-indulgent or decadent.

Hemingway would not defend his position—he was not going to defend anything he did—but he would explain something about the writer's responsibility as he saw it. He used in his letters and conversations about literature the world-weary tone of the veteran, an expert by virtue of experience. He did not need to be lectured about politics: he'd seen it from the inside as a reporter and journalist, both in America and in Europe. All politics was the same, each brand hiding under a different name. Politics was the worst thing for a writer to get involved in because it was the writer's greatest duty to find absolute reality and truth, and then re-create them on the page. There was no reality in politics: it was like a bog whose features kept constantly shifting. Nothing changed, and certainly men could change nothing.

John Dos Passos, always intensely political, had lately turned polemical on the page. He was making speeches, Hemingway said, not creating art. Dos Passos, he argued, should listen to Hemingway. "For Christ sake don't try to do good. Keep on showing it as it is. If you can show it as it really is you will do good. If you try to do good you'll not do any good nor will you show it." The art itself was what mattered, and after that the quality of each day's life. Writing was the hardest work in the world, and time away from the desk should be spent at equally hard play, not politics.

While Dos Passos and others were pamphleteering, as he saw it, Hemingway was appearing more prominently than ever in the country's top magazines. If *Scribner's Magazine* consistently annoyed him by refusing stories their readers might find objectionable, there were other magazines that would pay more for Hemingway at his most brutal and realistic. The name Ernest Hemingway on the cover meant increased sales. It was a name found on marquees as well. A theatrical adaptation of *A Farewell to Arms* had failed at the box office, but a motion picture starring Gary Cooper and Helen Hayes had done quite well. The film's trivializing of the relationship between Lieutenant Henry and Catherine Barkley angered Hemingway nearly as much as the happy ending created on a soundstage. It all proved to Hemingway that Hollywood was as bad for writers as was politics. The only thing the motion picture industry was good for was money, although Hemingway found himself interested in an offer to serve as adviser for a documentary about Spain. Otherwise his work was meant for type and paper, not celluloid.

With *Winner Take Nothing* nearly complete, Hemingway began casting about for a new project. His knowledge of marlin and of marlin fishing had become encyclopedic. He had studied the fish as a scientist, caught them as a sportsman, sold them commercially alongside fishermen. He understood their habits and was almost obsessed with their habitat, the waters of the Gulf Stream. Many called the Gulf Stream the biggest river in the world, but even that was too trivial a description. Landscape and terrain had always spoken clearly to Hemingway; sense of place was perhaps the strongest of his strong senses. The Gulf Stream had its own terrain, was itself a landscape, and the marlin that swam deep beneath it or leapt high above it were its proudest creatures. Hemingway planned a book on marlin and the Gulf Stream, an explication of sportfishing as ambitious and innovative as *Death in the Afternoon*. It could be a great work, one that would take years.

A new magazine had more immediate use for Hemingway's knowledge, not to mention his name. *Esquire,* a men's quarterly magazine, would make its appearance in the fall of 1933. The magazine, according to its editor and founder Arnold Gingrich, would be devoted to the finer things in men's life. Fashion would play a major part in the contents, but there was plenty of room for more adventurous topics. It would be the perfect place for Hemingway to appear. Gingrich could not afford Hemingway's fiction, but he offered $250 apiece for Hemingway's commentaries on game fishing and hunting.

"Marlin Off the Morro: A Cuban Letter" was Hemingway's title for his first *Esquire* piece. He described the sport as he knew it, explaining not only the best way to use the power of a fishing boat to tow bait, but also the sort of breakfast that best served the marlin fisherman. On days when he was going after marlin, Hemingway kept his enormous appetite in check, eating only a thick slice of Cuban bread and drinking only milk and soda water. His big meal would be lunch, served deliciously at sea, a feast to follow the landing of one or more marlin.

Hemingway felt comfortable with the brief article form, and increased his production when *Esquire* became a monthly magazine. He had plenty to write about for *Esquire*'s audience: the

African safari was becoming a reality. Gus Pfeiffer's fortunes had improved during 1933, the offer of financing was renewed, and Hemingway began to assemble a crew for the trip. During the years of planning for the expedition, Hemingway had acquired suitable rifles and an arsenal of knowledge from memoirs and magazines. Now he was eager to test his studies against the realities of Africa. Charles Thompson of Key West would be accompanying him, but Mike Strater and others who had been invited were unable to go along. Finally Hemingway gave in to Pauline's request that she join him on safari. Ursula Hemingway was summoned from Oak Park to care for Patrick and Gregory during the months Hemingway and Pauline would be away.

They sailed for Paris in August. Adding to Hemingway's happiness was the news that Hadley had fallen in love and remarried. Her new husband was Paul Scott Mowrer, an American journalist whom Hemingway had known casually in Paris. It was a good match and Hemingway wished the couple the very best. There was still no one on earth finer than Hadley, and in his own way he would love her for the rest of his life.

By November 1933, the Hemingways and Charles Thompson were embarked from France on their voyage to Africa. Hemingway hurried to finish a last piece of writing before the safari began. He had been experimenting with a new protagonist, Harry Morgan, a boat owner and rumrunner fashioned after Hemingway's notion of a pirate. He completed a long Harry Morgan story and sent it to *Cosmopolitan.* The time had come to put serious writing away for a while, and to begin gathering the serious experiences from which such writing was built. Hemingway was moving into another territory and he intended to experience it fully, to absorb as well as he could the sights, sounds, incidents—the wildlife and countryside—of Africa.

The new continent opened itself to them daily. They put into Port Said in Egypt and Hemingway studied its citizens and architecture as though he were a student. During the passage through the Suez Canal he would not leave the rail; he hunched over it and watched the landscape pass by. The ship's itinerary took them through the Red Sea, the Gulf of Aden, and then down the long west coast of Africa to Mombasa, the island port through which they would enter Kenya. The safari itself was to be organized at a farm outside Nairobi, three hundred miles inland by train. The rails rose steadily up from sea level, climbing more than five thousand feet through stunning countryside. The spaciousness of Africa seized Hemingway and his imagination; in some places the hills and sky seemed to go on forever. He was reminded both of the American West and of parts of New England. Africa's beauty had made him impatient to get on with the adventure, although the altitude gave him some difficulty in sustaining his usual high-speed pace.

The farm at which the Hemingway party gathered was owned by Philip Percival, the white hunter engaged to guide them on safari. Percival had been born in England but had been in Africa for nearly three decades. At forty-nine, gray-haired and unflappable, Percival was both a successful farmer and a famous, respected guide. In addition to fruit and coffee, cattle and horses, the Percival farm raised ostriches for their harvest of plumes. Years before, Percival helped guide Theodore Roosevelt through Africa; now, his expertise and ability to teach immediately earned him Hemingway's total respect. Percival made clear the seriousness of the hunt they were about to undertake, explaining to the safari party the rules by which a proper kill was earned. For his part, Hemingway listened carefully, learned quickly, and abandoned his vanity. He kept his glasses on constantly to ensure the accuracy of his shots.

Five days before Christmas 1933, they set out. On that first day they traveled nearly two hundred miles, the hunters and their gunbearers riding in an open Rover, their tents and gear in two trucks that followed. Although their first night was spent in a hotel in sight of Mount Kilimanjaro, by their second evening they were camped beneath enormous green trees next to a fast, clear stream. As they pushed farther into Tanganyika, Hemingway got better acquainted with Percival's African crew. He took their measure, and his own against it, learning quickly who was the best hunter, who the most skilled tracker. He tried to understand the hierarchy of rank and prestige among the Africans as he had among matadors or soldiers. To some of the bearers Hemingway assigned nicknames such as "Droopy." Others, and especially the bearer M'Cola, made clear their disinterest in wealthy white people who became hunters for a few weeks. It was clear they that the white hunters had to prove themselves. The only exception was Pauline Hemingway, the only white woman along, who immediately became an object of the Africans' great respect and admiration.

Proving themselves, after all, was what they had come to Africa to accomplish, and it was Pauline, in fact, who was awarded the first lion. By the first week of January the party had enjoyed great success in hunting gazelle and many other kinds of antelope. They had also killed two leopards. It was not until late one afternoon, nearly at dark, that they came upon their first lion, a female. By agreement Pauline had the first shot. The lion took off, and Hemingway fired twice. One of his shots missed, but the other brought down the lioness, keeping her from escaping into the brush. The Africans saw it as Pauline's kill and hoisted her onto their shoulders. It was a small lie, to which the entire party acceded, but it gave Hemingway pause. It was the sort of thing that shifted relationships among a group. When he killed his own lion a few days afterward, the first thing Hemingway noticed was the size of the flies that instantly swarmed over the carcass.

For a while he thought he might himself die. The safari was hardly well begun when Hemingway began to suffer from amebic dysentery. He passed blood constantly and could not control his bowels, but insisted that he would not abandon the hunt. By the middle of January 1934, he was weak from loss of blood and thin from loss of weight. Hunting, he grew delirious, convinced that he was witnessing the coming of a Buddha who looked just like Gertrude Stein. By radio a biplane was called, and Hemingway was strapped into the rear seat for the flight to the hospital at Nairobi. Hemingway's lower intestine had collapsed, slipping out of position. A doctor prescribed emetine, which worked so quickly that Hemingway requested writing materials. He used his time in bed to write another brief piece for *Esquire*. He described his amebic dysentery, the scenery, and the four lions killed by that time.

By January 23, when he rejoined the group, they had moved up off the plain and were in pursuit of sable and rhinocerous. Hemingway felt better daily. He hunted for long hours and then relaxed over whiskey beside the campfire, talking with Philip Percival and Charles Thompson. They told stories, compared hunting techniques, debated the nature of courage. Hemingway remained alert for material, and drew Percival out about his former clients, the countryside, incidents and anecdotes. Each was fascinating, perhaps none more so than the tale of a mountain climber's assault on Kilimanjaro, which rose nearly four miles and whose Kibo Peak was permanently snow-covered. The climber found, frozen in the snow, the carcass of a leopard. Hemingway had flown near Kilimanjaro en route to the hospital, and the story of the leopard on the mountain delighted him.

He grew less pleased with the hunting. He killed kudu, buffalo, zebra, and rhinoceros, but his trophies were not so large as Charles Thompson's, and the sport seemed almost safe. Buffalo moved much less rapidly than a matador's bull; zebra were good only for their hides; the rhinoceros was, despite its speed, something of a joke. None of the animals offered the danger he'd come in search of, none seemed threatening, many were easy to hit. Hemingway's mind returned to the lion, to leopards so swift that a shotgun was the only sensible weapon. His theories of hunting grew more complex. "There are two ways to murder a lion," he wrote for *Esquire*. "One is to shoot him from a motor car, the other, to shoot him at night . . . as he comes to feed on a bait placed by the shootist or his guide. . . . These two ways to murder lion rank, as sport, with dynamiting trout or harpooning swordfish." The test was in the stalk. "In the ethics of shooting dangerous game is the premise that the trouble you shoot yourself into you must be prepared to shoot yourself out of," he wrote. Things had to be done properly. "If you shoot as you should on the Serengeti, having the car drive off as you get out, the chances are that the first shot will be a moving shot. . . . That means that unless you are a good or a very lucky shot there will be a wounded lion and a possible charge. . . . It will be exactly as dangerous as you choose to make it." Courage meant making the situation as dangerous as possible while maintaining the steady hand and eye needed to shoot well. Done properly, game hunting placed great pressure upon the hunter, whose success could be measured by the grace and skill he displayed.

The safari ended in February and, if Hemingway never found a situation in which his life was in danger, the quality of his trophies had at least improved. Everyone agreed that Hemingway's kudu were the most impressive of all, the prize of the safari with horns that curled several feet upward. They seemed more like beautiful ironwork than part of an animal.

As the group returned to Nairobi, Hemingway's thoughts were full of the country he'd seen, its people, their legends, the life that surrounded them. He wanted to come back as soon as possible, and spoke of an expedition after elephant, which he wanted to make in 1935. He continued to work out his theory of hunting, his code of courage and conduct. Already he was beginning to use his new ideas and perceptions in his writing, but the *Esquire* pieces were little more than dress rehearsals for a more ambitious project. He was eager to attempt for African big game hunting what he felt he'd accomplished for the bullfight. He wanted to write another nonfiction book, this one a narrative of his safari. Ideas flowed, but the work would have to wait until he was back in his new workroom in Key West. For now, having been for so many weeks in debt to Philip Percival's expertise and areas of special knowledge, Hemingway wanted to show off his own. He chartered a rickety boat and took Percival sportfishing off the African coast.

TWELVE

PILAR

APRIL 1934 WAS HEMINGWAY'S first full month in Key West since the previous July. There was a great deal to catch up on. It had been half a year since he and Pauline had seen their sons, and they marveled at how the boys had grown. Hemingway settled easily into his workroom, spending the earliest hours of the day writing in pencil at a small table. The afternoons were reserved for fishing; his trips grew longer and longer as he investigated the Gulf Stream and the area's islands. He watched the ways captains handled the boats he chartered. In New York, on the last leg of his return from Africa, he'd made a down payment on a vessel of his own. While he was overseas, his story of Harry Morgan, "One Trip Across," had sold to *Cosmopolitan* for more than $5,000. Hemingway's articles had proved so popular that Arnold Gingrich advanced him $3,000 on pieces yet unwritten. With his work earning such sums, Hemingway felt the expense of a boat justified and paid Gingrich's advance to the Wheeler Shipyard of Brooklyn.

He knew what he wanted. When finished to Hemingway's special instructions, the boat would be nothing less than a fishing machine, able to sleep seven, cruise five hundred miles, make sixteen knots in smooth seas and handle well in rough ones. At the stern of the boat he had the transom removed and a wooden roller installed to facilitate the landing of big fish. The galley would gleam with chrome, the trim was polished mahogany, and the housing and thirty-eight-foot hull would be painted jet black. There had never been anything like her and he named her after a Spanish shrine: *Pilar.*

Despite his anticipation, which built throughout the month of the *Pilar's* construction, Hemingway worked hard at his African book. Where *Death in the Afternoon* had been a rumination on bullfighting, the new book would have the pace and feel of a novel. He had injected himself into the bullfight book as a commentator, but in *The Highlands of Africa,* as he called the new work, he would be narrator, the central character of the story. He wrote of the Africans under the names by which he'd known them—M'Cola, Droopy—and for the others in the party he invented nicknames. Pauline became Poor Old Mama, or P.O.M., Philip Percival became Pop, Charles Thompson was known as Karl. He wrote and rewrote the opening pages of the book, looking for the words that would take the reader to Africa, make the reader see and feel what Hemingway had seen and felt.

When the *Pilar* arrived in Miami in early May, Hemingway put aside the manuscript and raced to pick up his boat. She was even more beautiful than he'd expected, and he displayed the boat proudly at the dock in Key West. At first he took short cruises, getting to know the boat, coming to understand how to handle her in every type of water. He took his brother Leicester out and offered advice on fishing and manhood. Arnold Samuelson, a would-be writer, came to Key West to ask Hemingway's advice and found himself nicknamed "Maestro" and hired as deckhand. With ichthyologists from Philadelphia's Academy of Natural Sciences, Hemingway took the *Pilar* on more than a month of trips to marlin habitats. The scientists learned so much that they began a revision of the system by which marlin were classified. Unable to find a permanent crew for the *Pilar* in her first season, Hemingway carried friends, writers, boxers, painters, bartenders—men, women, and children. His delight in his boat seemed as innocent as a child's, and he wanted to share it.

In his workroom he alternated between the African book and pieces for *Esquire.* He wrote quickly for Gingrich, open letters on a variety of subjects. He expounded on the proper way to fish for marlin, just as he'd explained game hunting. He wrote of politics, journalism, literature. One open letter, "Defense of Dirty Words," gave him the opportunity to respond to his critics, who accused him of taking a small boy's pleasure in the use of shocking language or incidents. That was nonsense, Hemingway wrote: what he took pleasure in was the re-creation of life as he had seen and heard it. If his characters employed dirty language on the page it was because they were equally obscene in real life. If their behavior seemed immoral, perhaps that was a problem that rested more properly with those who believed in set standards of moral behavior. Again he was trying to make the point he'd argued throughout his career—he belonged to no school of fashionable thought, subscribed to no formal system of belief. He believed in what he saw.

By fall he had re-created what he had seen in Africa, finishing his book not long before Thanksgiving. It was, Hemingway thought, nothing less than wonderful, as good as any novel and even better because it was true. He now called the book *Green Hills of Africa,* and gave some thought to publishing it as the opening section of a complete collection of his short stories. Although Hemingway at thirty-five seemed to some too young for such a retrospective, he felt the time was absolutely right. There were more than fifty stories, a large book in itself. The addition of the full-length African narrative would make the book massive. The public would welcome such a collection, and the achievement it displayed would also show his critics a thing or two. No other writer on earth could do what Hemingway could do. No other writer had such a portfolio, and he wanted to show it off.

Maxwell Perkins agreed with Hemingway's attitude toward the value of his work as art. Publishing, though, was a business, and he saw little commercial prospect for *Green Hills of Africa.* It would sell, certainly, but not so well as a novel. After much arguing he persuaded Hemingway to accept from *Scribner's*

Magazine an advance that was smaller than *Cosmopolitan's* payment for a single short story. Men of letters tended to have smaller incomes than novelists—fiction, Perkins explained, was not only Hemingway's proper domain, it was his most profitable. The best large book Hemingway could produce now would be a novel.

Hemingway hardly had time. The *belle epoque* that had yielded *Green Hills of Africa,* and a nearly monthly series of *Esquire* articles, was now receding. What he needed after such hard work was activity that would renew his creative energies. At 210 pounds he also looked forward to getting his body back into good shape. Fortunately the spring of 1935, the arrival of the game-fishing season, and the *Pilar* were present beyond the door of his workroom. They offered all the distraction he required. Since he would not be returning to Africa this year, he planned an ambitious marlin expedition, virtually a safari at sea. For four months his base of operations would be the small island of Bimini in the Bahamas, more than two hundred miles northeast of Key West, fifty miles off Miami.

This year's crew included John and Katy Dos Passos, Mike Strater, and several others. Hemingway put to sea early in April and, unwilling to wait, began fishing before Key West had faded from the horizon. Shark were running, and Hemingway hooked and boated a large one. The fish still had a great deal of life left, and Hemingway drew a pistol and began firing at the shark's head. The pitch of the boat threw his aim off. One of his bullets struck a metal cleat, split into fragments, and ricocheted into Hemingway's legs. He collapsed, vomiting, and the party returned to Key West. Hemingway turned the incident into a piece for *Esquire,* explaining incidentally the proper way of killing a shark at sea, giving a medical description of his wounds, and outlining his plans for the Bimini trip. They sailed a week after the accident.

Bimini in 1935 was a quiet, virtually unknown island. Its link to the mainland was by boat or seaplane; there was no airport. The beaches shone a brilliant white, and the islanders' shacks looked as they might have in the days of pirates, centuries before. There were rough bars in which to have a drink, a wharf at which to secure the *Pilar*. Best of all, the island rose out of the dark Gulf Stream in the center of some of the world's finest fishing. Once again, Hemingway was home.

Since Bimini was to be at least his temporary home, Hemingway wasted no time establishing himself as the island's master. He bought a tommy gun, which he claimed would be more effective on sharks than a pistol. More than once he was caught sleeping with the machine gun held close, always ready for action. Hemingway was also quick to remind others that he did not need firearms to win a battle. Insulted by a drunk at the dock, Hemingway gave the man a sound beating, learning only later that the drunk was an influential magazine publisher. It was, he said, one way of restricting one's markets. The publisher admitted starting the fight and apologized, and the islanders delighted Hemingway by composing a calypso song about his exploits. They sang it on the beaches at night, and Hemingway made a standing offer of $250 to any local black who could beat him in a fistfight. There were several takers, the bouts always gathered a crowd, and Hemingway never lost.

By August Hemingway was back in Key West, weight down and creative energy up. The marlin book remained in his mind and scattered in notes throughout his workroom, but he did not want to do another nonfiction book. At the same time he had no firm plans for a novel. He was attracted to the idea of writing about the Civil War, but made no serious start. As fall neared, he began another story of Harry Morgan, his rumrunner who reminded him of pirates. Hemingway also worked hard preparing his house, and especially *Pilar*, for the coming hurricane season.

When the first storm of 1935 struck, it was the worst the Keys had ever witnessed. The *Pilar* came through the hurricane undamaged, but there were rumors of great devastation to the north. Before the seas were calm, Hemingway took the *Pilar* to

Lower Matecumbe Key to see if he could be of assistance to the Civilian Conservation Corps workers billeted there. There were thousands of workers, veterans given construction jobs as part of President Roosevelt's New Deal.

As he reached the island, Hemingway realized that the rumors could not even hint at the size of the disaster brought by the hurricane. The island had been stripped of vegetation, and every building had vanished. Machinery lay buried in the sand. There were bodies everywhere, decomposing, as covered with flies as the lion he'd shot the year before. These bodies, though, had belonged to brave veterans who'd only sought to work during the depression. Hemingway recognized some of the victims, local girls—a rummy, he called one of them—acquaintances. He'd not seen anything like this since the explosion of the ammunition factory in Italy nearly two decades before. The locals understood the weather and knew the risks they took living on the Keys during the hurricane season. The veterans, though, had gone only where Roosevelt's CCC had told them to go. The administration, as Hemingway saw it, was clearly guilty.

He said so publicly in a piece for *New Masses,* a socialist journal that had taken Hemingway to task for his lack of political commitment. "Who Murdered the Vets?" was the title of Hemingway's article, and in its pages he pulled no punches answering his own question. The political left, which had been so quick to criticize Hemingway's apathy, as they saw it, now rushed to praise his new sense of social conscience. "Who Murdered the Vets?" Hemingway argued angrily, was no evidence of any change, certainly not of a swing to the left. The article was just the truth, which was all he cared about or had ever cared about. He wrote the piece because he had been to Lower Matecumbe Key and seen the truth firsthand, as he always did. That, he felt, was a larger claim to commitment than any left-wing writer could make.

In his workroom after the storm he returned to his own concerns. He finished "The Tradesman's Return," his new Harry

Morgan story. He had ideas for a few more stories about the rumrunner, and now thought of them as the proper introduction to a complete collection. He began the third story not long before New Year's, 1936. It was growing harder to work in Key West—not only was the island growing more populous, it was attracting increasing numbers of tourists. Hemingway's own celebrity was still increasing, and visitors thought nothing of interrupting his work to ask foolish questions or request autographs. Some of the books they brought him to sign were not even his own. He regretted that he could not beat every tourist or politician or movie star who intruded upon his privacy. He did manage to punch the poet Wallace Stevens, who was in Key West on vacation and had said some critical words about Hemingway's artistic vision.

Stevens was not the only critic Hemingway wanted to hit. *Green Hills of Africa* had received the worst reviews of his career. Some thought that it was merely a poor book, but others brought Hemingway's character into question. When had the he-man masculinity begun to seem overbearing? Was Hemingway a bully? Why was he so fascinated with death—with the mechanics of death and killing? The opinions seemed in some ways to echo Grace Hemingway's attitudes about writers' responsibilities, and Hemingway dismissed his critics as easily as he had dismissed his mother: they didn't have the strength or stomach to face reality. As for himself, he could face anything. He had enough strength left after a six-hour battle against a five-hundred-pound tuna to hang the twelve-foot fish over the Key West dock and use it drunkenly as a punching bag.

His refusal to make a public defense of his behavior remained constant, although in private conversations and letters Hemingway could go on obscenely for hours or pages about his right to do exactly as he pleased. The quality of his work earned him that right. He worked hard in the early hours every morning, paying closer attention to his prose than anyone could imagine. A good day's work was three or four hundred words, a slow and exacting rate. Writing was hard labor, it hurt, but the results were worth it. During the spring and summer of 1936, in addition to his new Harry Morgan story, Hemingway wrote two long stories that he thought not only the best he'd ever accomplished, but also among the world's very best.

His mind was on Africa once more and, since he was again unable to make a safari, he returned to the continent in fiction. "The Happy Ending" was the first of his African stories, telling of Francis and Margot Macomber and their pursuit of big game. Hemingway captured the countryside and the sense of the hunt even more effectively than in *Green Hills of Africa,* and was able in fiction to focus more closely than ever on the question of courage. Charged by a wounded lion, Francis Macomber panics and runs. His own attitude toward his cowardice, his wife's disgust, their white hunter's attempt to understand the couple—all work together through Hemingway's art to create a story whose tension grows to a stunning, violent climax. Before submission he changed the title to "The Short Happy Life of Francis Macomber," under which it appeared in the September 1936 issue of *Cosmopolitan.*

The second of his African stories probed even more deeply into the nature of courage and the qualities of character that make a worthwhile life. As he was writing the story, Hemingway called it "A Budding Friendship," and realized that he had set himself one of the most demanding technical challenges of his career. His protagonist was a dying writer stranded by engine failure in the shadow of Mount Kilimanjaro. As the gangrene that developed as a result of a scratch takes more and more of his life, the writer's thoughts travel back through his personal history, pausing on the good moments, lingering over the little defeats and surrenders that he'd made, trading the possibility of worthwhile work for comfort and wealth. High above, on Kilimanjaro's frozen peak, lies the corpse of the leopard that had not ceased to climb. It was, Hemingway boasted, some job: there was enough detail and insight in the story to make four whole novels from a lesser writer. Again he changed the title before publication, and it appeared in *Esquire* as "The Snows of Kilimanjaro."

One result of this story, which was hailed immediately as a masterpiece, was the final break in Hemingway's friendship with F. Scott Fitzgerald. Fitzgerald's career had collapsed; his last novel, *Tender Is the Night*, had not done well; Zelda was regularly institutionalized with increasingly serious psychological disorders. As Hemingway's writer lies dying, he thinks with contempt of poor Fitzgerald's "romantic awe" of the rich and how Fitzgerald "thought they were a special glamorous race and when he found they weren't it wrecked him just as much as any other thing that wrecked him." Hurt, Fitzgerald objected, and in subsequent publications of the story Hemingway substituted a fictional name, and sprang on occasion to Fitzgerald's defense. He thought, however, that Fitzgerald's complaint was one more sign of the writer's failure of nerve.

The success of his two African stories convinced Hemingway that publication of a complete collection of his short fiction was vital. He wanted to bounce back from the bad reviews with some good ones, and thought of placing the Harry Morgan stories at the front of the collection. The Morgan stories were virtually a novel in themselves and would make an impressive introduction to his collected work. Maxwell Perkins agreed with Hemingway, but pointed out that no story collection would be as impressive as a new novel. Nearly eight years had passed since publication of *A Farewell to Arms*, and there were those who said that Hemingway did not have another novel in him. Perkins's opinion was echoed by others, and after some deliberation Hemingway began recasting the Morgan stories as a self-contained book.

His attention was distracted by somber news from Spain. On July 18, 1936, General Francisco Franco and other military officers led a revolt against the Popular Front Republican Government and its socialist policies. The Nationalists, as Franco and his troops were called, were well armed, the rebellion became a civil war, and by the end of the year Franco and his forces were in command of most of southern Spain. The Republicans fought bravely against Franco, and began to receive military aid from the Soviet Union. Volunteers from around the world who supported the Republican cause formed international brigades, giving their courage, money, and lives to the struggle. Franco found assistance of his own from Fascist Italy and Nazi Germany. The Spanish Civil War was a war of ideologies, left against right, socialist against fascist.

For all his talk about the emptiness of politics, Hemingway followed the news from Spain almost obsessively, telling his friends that instead of writing novels he should be fighting alongside the Republicans. Dos Passos was there, along with other writers, artists, and intellectuals who felt that Spain was the place where their beliefs could be turned into action. It was a place to take a stand. Hemingway began pressing newspapers for a journalistic assignment that would provide him with the credentials needed legitimately to enter Spain, and at the same time be sufficiently lucrative to fit his status as a major writer. He needed the money, having gone into debt to donate an ambulance to the Spanish cause.

The assignment he accepted came from the North American Newspaper Alliance, which would syndicate his dispatches to more than sixty newspapers. The offer was startling, a fee of $500 for stories sent by cable, $1,000 for reports long enough to send by mail. It averaged nearly a dollar a word, and was one more incentive for Hemingway to get to the front as quickly as possible.

He would not leave until he completed the Harry Morgan novel. Hemingway called the novel *To Have and Have Not* and in it contrasted the rough life of rumrunner Harry Morgan and the lives of a variety of wealthy socialites and drunken artists in and around Key West. The tone of *To Have and Have Not* was more hard-boiled and masculine than anything he'd previously written, with Morgan's uncompromising independence seeming to consolidate in a single character all of Hemingway's beliefs: Morgan had no interest in politics, Morgan was ready to fight, he fished, he used guns, he could outdrink anyone, he did not complain even when he lost an arm. He needed no one.

But, with the conflict in Spain deepening and the world lurching toward another global war, Hemingway was beginning to realize that independence was not enough, nor was strength, nor courage. He wrestled with the problem on the page, seeking to come to terms with the causes and ideas around which others so readily rallied. He still was not ready to give his name to any cause, and his character Harry Morgan was even less ready. But, at the end of the book, as he lay dying from a gunshot wound, Morgan struggled to give voice to an idea new to him and perhaps equally new to his creator.

"'A man,' said Harry Morgan, very slowly. 'Ain't got no hasn't got any can't really isn't any way out.' He stopped. . . . 'One man alone ain't got. No man alone now.' He stopped. 'No matter how a man alone ain't got no bloody fucking chance.'

"He shut his eyes. It had taken him a long time to get it out and it had taken him all of his life to learn it."

It was no repudiation. Hemingway made that clear to friends who read the manuscript. In some ways it was just a restatement of everything he had said all along. Now he had said it even more brutally, using the freedom of language he had helped win for writers. Alone was the way everyone was—but alone no one had a chance. Harry Morgan's statement could be seen as a reworking of the *nada* creed. When the book's early readers told Hemingway they saw something more, a dawning social conscience, a sense of the need for community and fellowship, Hemingway shrugged them off. He was just trying to write the truth as he saw it.

With the novel completed, Hemingway turned his full attention to Spain. Early in 1937 he helped write narration for a fund-raising film, and talked with Dos Passos about another film.

Difficulties with visas kept him from Spain until March 1937, and it took him most of the month to reach Madrid. The Republicans had recently won a major victory over the Italian troops who supported Franco, and Hemingway hurried to the battlefield in order to see it before the bodies were removed. He had for some time been collecting photographs of corpses and corpse-strewn battlefields, storing them in stacks in his workroom. He was as amazed at thirty-seven by the grotesque positions of the dead as he had been when a teenager. The postures and expressions of the dead continued to fascinate Hemingway, and he used that fascination in his newspaper cables and stories.

Away from the front he stayed in Madrid, keeping company with other reporters and writers. Madrid was under heavy bombardment from Franco's artillery, and Hemingway showed the others the proper attitude of fearlessness to display when under siege. He knew of war, was an old warrior himself; and if the others would listen to him they would all do fine. The air was full of dust and smoke: Hemingway breathed it in as though it were a special perfume. Bullets sang overhead: Hemingway showed others the safest way to lie on the ground. As the shelling of Madrid grew heavier, some of the tenants worried about a direct hit on their hotel, the Florida. Hemingway made a speech in which he proved that, because of the angle at which the hotel faced, it was impossible for the building to be struck. He had barely finished when an artillery shell hit the hotel: Hemingway smiled, did not miss a breath, and yanked the others to their feet, offering them drinks from a silver flask. Broad script on the side of the flask read *To EH from EH.* He was having a wonderful time.

He was not having it alone. Also in Madrid to cover the war was Martha Gellhorn, a writer in her twenties who was serving as a special correspondent for *Collier's.* Hemingway had met Martha Gellhorn the previous December, when she and her mother passed through Key West. She had already published a novel, *What Mad Pursuit,* and a book of short stories, *The*

Trouble I've Seen. She'd been reviewed favorably and her collection had borne an introduction by H. G. Wells. Impressed with Hemingway, she had lingered in Key West, been introduced to Pauline and the children, drunk with Hemingway and discussed her writing, listened to his opinions and pronouncements. They agreed to meet in Spain, although their reunion was spoiled by Hemingway's claiming credit for her credentials. She was a thoroughgoing professional writer, driven by her own ambitions and abilities, with her own portfolio, and she had made her way to Spain on her own. Tall, blonde, and striking, she reminded Hemingway and others of a movie star. They called her Marty.

Outside the Florida the war went on. From the windows of the hotel the correspondents and photographers could often see dead and wounded lying in the streets of Madrid. Hemingway was fascinated by the way Madrid's dogs, once pets, now scurried to the bodies in the street in search of food. That image was one face of war, he maintained, that once seen could never be forgotten.

Inside the hotel there was some respite. Hemingway became the object of envy because of the privileges granted him due to his status and celebrity. Hemingway had relatively unlimited gasoline and food, and almost unlimited supplies of liquor. As less well known correspondents rose each morning to scrounge a meal, the odor of fresh ham and eggs drifted from the suite Hemingway shared with Sidney Franklin. Often Hemingway would appear at the head of the stairs and, like a grinning giant, invite the others up to share his meal. His rooms were strewn with maps and military rosters, and as they ate and drank Hemingway discoursed on strategy, tactics, and the inevitability of a Republican victory over the fascists.

From Madrid he filed stories in which he attempted to give his readers a sense of the Spanish Civil War as he saw it. He wrote of his feelings upon seeing so many Italian dead—they were the enemy now, but he could never forget that he had stood in World War I beside other Italian soldiers. In one piece he talked of the Spanish chauffeurs who carried him to the front. In another he wrote of the kind of war this was, a new kind of war, a testing ground for theories of warfare and technologies of warfare that had developed since 1918, a war in which there was no glory, no medals, only wounds.

During the course of his first stay in Spain, Hemingway and Martha Gellhorn became lovers. They managed to keep their relationship secret until the night another shell struck the Florida and they emerged into the smoke from the same room. Dos Passos and others then in Spain also knew Pauline, and were fond of her, but their advice to Hemingway went unheeded. He was in love again and it was as though it were the first time.

By April, documentary filmmaking was uppermost in Hemingway's mind, and the frequency of his dispatches slowed. He used his prestige to get permission to film at the front, and in company with his camera crew sought to capture in a motion picture the essence of the Spanish Civil War. He was not after action alone. The film would be called *The Spanish Earth*, and Hemingway would write the narration for it. The film must show not only the effect of the war on the people of Spain, but also the character of the war as it was taking shape. He followed tank groups as they moved into place, made clear that the new machine guns were a considerable advance over those used twenty years earlier, caught the devastation caused by modern aircraft bombardment. By early May he had enough footage, and was in New York by the middle of the month. A rough editing had the film in shape to be shown early in June.

One of the first places *The Spanish Earth* was shown was at the Second American Writers' Congress in New York. Hemingway was one of the speakers at the gathering of writers; he was to show the film. Others on the dais addressed the question of Spain, calling loudly for involvement on the Republican side of the struggle by every American writer: it was the writer's responsibility to aid this cause. Hemingway let the film speak for

Spain, and spoke himself of his one constant concern and belief—the writer's responsibility to seek the truth and re-create
the truth on each page he wrote. Writers must write so well that
their truth became the reader's, he said again. That sort of work
was impossible under fascism, and for that reason writers must
oppose the ambitions of the fascist powers. Offstage he would
argue that no piece written primarily as propaganda could be
great art, no matter how noble its cause. Art and truth must
come first, above all else.

Hemingway had proved himself ready to face danger in the
cause of art, and in August 1937 he demonstrated the dangers
critics might face in the cause of criticizing Hemingway. He'd
had a busy spring and summer, touring with *The Spanish Earth,*
speaking for the Spanish cause. With Martha Gellhorn he dined
at the White House with the Roosevelts. In one evening he
raised nearly $20,000 for Spanish aid. As summer ended he was
preparing to return to Spain, stopping briefly in New York to
take care of final pre-publication details regarding his new
novel. In Maxwell Perkins's office he encountered the critic Max
Eastman, who four years earlier had written a review entitled
"Bull in the Afternoon," accusing Hemingway of false masculinity. For a few moments the atmosphere in the office was cordial
but Hemingway soon began sparring verbally with Eastman,
pressing the critic about his own masculinity. Hemingway
opened his shirt and revealed the thick growth of hair on his
chest; when he opened Eastman's shirt, he saw nothing but bare
skin. Without warning Hemingway grabbed a book—a volume
of Eastman's essays—and hit Max Eastman with it. Eastman hit
back, the two fell to the floor, and when Perkins broke up the
fight Eastman was on top.

In a statement released to the press Eastman took credit for
beating Ernest Hemingway in a fair fight. Hemingway, about to
sail for Europe, offered his own public response, not only deny-
ing that he had been beaten but also challenging Eastman to a
rematch in a locked room. If Eastman could beat Hemingway

under such circumstances, no holds barred, Hemingway said, he would give $1,000 to charity. He took a further moment to show the press his scars, then boarded the *Champlain* for his return to real combat.

THIRTEEN

CELEBRITY

THE WAR IN SPAIN was going poorly for the Republicans. Less than a third of the country remained under their control. Occasional dramatic victories kept hope kindled, but many observers were beginning to concede the inevitability of Franco's victory. Hemingway, reunited with Martha Gellhorn, traveled deep into Aragon, sometimes on horseback, sometimes walking, living with the peasants, struggling to find food and keep warm. They shared the deprivations stoically, as though guerilla fighters themselves, and Hemingway fell more deeply in love with her. Her professionalism and her courage were a match for his, he felt, and most who knew them agreed.

As fall neared, Hemingway was once more installed in the Hotel Florida in Madrid, opening his doors, larder, and liquor supply to correspondents and soldiers alike. His quarters were always crowded, and he was at the center of the crowd, holding forth with matchless expertise on any topic that arose, from bullfighting to celestial navigation. Nothing fired his vehemence so much as talking about literary critics who, even as he spoke, were calling *To Have and Have Not* the weakest of his three novels. Not even a cover story in *Time* could calm him. Some of the critics said he was through as a writer, unable to break any new ground. Hemingway was too far removed from New York to respond with his fists, and undertook instead a literary counteroffensive.

He began writing a play set in a Madrid hotel during the Spanish Civil War. Those to whom he showed the manuscript in progress immediately recognized Hemingway as the heroic protagonist, and Martha Gellhorn as the female lead. The play took shape quickly—it would be a full-scale drama of intrigue and romance under the shadow of war, a three-act triumph in one of the most difficult media of all. The play would show everyone that Ernest Hemingway was far from finished. By late October the first draft was done and Hemingway was thinking of a double victory. Theatrical production alone was not enough: Scribners could publish the play, called *The Fifth Column,* as the introduction to the long-postponed collected stories. A hit on Broadway and a fat book on the best-seller lists would be a knockout combination no one could ignore.

Hemingway continued to file stories for the North American Newspaper Alliance. His dispatches took on more and more of a literary tone, some of them seeming virtual short stories, capturing a scene, a character, a bit of dialogue. When he restricted himself to straight journalistic reporting, the results often fell flat. His editors requested that he concentrate on human interest pieces, at which he excelled, but it had been a long time since an editor could tell Hemingway how to write his copy. He wrote as he pleased, passed Christmas in Spain with Martha, and early in 1938 returned to Paris.

Pauline was waiting for him there; the reunion was bitter. She had come to Europe in hopes of gaining permission to visit the Spanish front. It was as though she wanted to show Hemingway that Martha Gellhorn was not the only woman who possessed courage. Hemingway was unimpressed; he knew already that his second marriage was over, that Martha was the true love of his life now. Still, he returned to Key West with Pauline and attempted to settle into a productive domestic routine. He'd spent nearly six months in Spain, but he had not even reached the United States before he was planning another trip to the war. Pauline could not understand, no matter how he tried to explain to her: the war was where he belonged, it was where he was most fully alive. He sought distraction by serving as a referee for boxing matches, but that was hardly exciting after Spain. By early April 1938, he was back in Europe.

This time he stayed barely six weeks. He joined Martha, toured the front, began to admit that the Republican cause was hopeless. Germany was deeply involved in the war now, Luftwaffe dive-bombers perfecting deadly new tactics against helpless Spanish and Russian troops. Hemingway had finally seen enough of Spain and its civil war. In his final articles he presented the Spanish Civil War as a prelude to another European conflict, an entire continent in flames again. There was nothing to be done about it, and Hemingway's opinion was that the United States should not try to do anything about it. The best course to follow, he told his readers, was neutrality. Failing that, we should limit our involvement to selling weapons to the Allies at a profit. It was, he wrote, the attitude of a realist.

When summer arrived, he was ready for some relaxation and took Pauline and the boys to Wyoming for the hunting season. He spent his mornings preparing his collected short stories for publication. *The Fifth Column* would lead off the collection, followed by forty-nine short stories ranging from "Up in Michigan" from the beginning of his career to "Old Man at the Bridge," one of the dispatches he'd filed from Spain. In his introduction to the volume, he wrote of the writer's discipline, saying that it was his duty to seek experience until his talent became dulled by it. But then it was his responsibility to communicate his experience to the reader, resharpening his talent through long sessions at his desk. Hemingway closed his preface with a statement of intent: "I would like to live long enough to write three more novels and twenty-five more stories. I know some pretty good ones."

He was putting his Spanish experience to the test already. In addition to "Old Man at the Bridge" he wrote "The Butterfly and the Tank" and "The Denunciation," short stories based on incidents he'd witnessed. He'd already written a play set in Spain, and he was beginning to think that there was a novel among the material he'd gathered. As 1938 drew to a close the Republican front began to collapse. Hemingway made a final hurried visit to Spain. The Republicans had fought bravely but now their cause was lost; there was nothing more he could do for them. He was home in time for Christmas with Pauline and his sons, although the marriage was past saving. Hemingway missed Martha badly, but was determined to maintain appearances so long as he remained married to Pauline. He found escape on board the *Pilar,* and vented his frustration by deriding the producers who were readying *The Fifth Column* for auditions and tryouts. The whole process annoyed Hemingway; it was no way for a writer to work. He was a novelist, he said, and he had several ideas for novels. Some of them would deal with subjects as complex as war, others with simple people in simple lives— peasants, the poor marlin fishermen of Cuba. When he was going well he could write about anything.

By March 28, 1939, when Madrid finally fell and the Spanish Civil War came to an end after nearly three years of fighting and a quarter of a million dead, Hemingway was well into a new novel. It had begun as another short story of the war but expanded quickly. He felt an excitement he had not felt since *A Farewell to Arms,* a sense of creative strength. He could tell before the month was out that this new book would be the big novel that he, and not incidentally his critics, had been waiting a decade for, a book large in scope and theme. He began the novel in the first person but shifted quickly to the third, setting his scene, trying to capture the essence of the Spanish experience in the rhythms of his prose. His protagonist was Robert Jordan, an American intellectual in Spain to serve the cause. Jordan has been given the assignment of destroying an important bridge; the demolition must coincide with a Russian offensive against the fascists.

"He lay flat on the brown, pine-needled floor of the forest, his chin on his folded arms, and high overhead the wind blew in the tops of the pine trees. The mountainside sloped gently where he lay; but below it was steep and he could see the dark of the oiled road winding through the pass. There was a stream alongside the road and far down the pass he saw a mill beside the stream and the falling water of the dam, white in the summer sunlight."

Jordan joins the camp of a band of partisans, guerilla fighters who live like foxes in caves in the hills. Hemingway established their character through dialogue, attempting to reproduce the Castilian dialect with which he was so taken. "'Art thou a brute? Yes. Art thou a beast? Yes, many times. Hast thou a brain? Nay. None. Now we come for something of consummate importance and thee, with thy dwelling place to be undisturbed, puts thy foxhole before the interests of humanity.'" The Spanish characters came to life quickly, Hemingway making each a vivid person. Among the partisan band were old Anselmo; Pablo, who was cynical and sullen in middle age; and most vivid of all, Pilar, the "woman of Pablo." Hemingway grew as fond of the character Pilar as of her namesake, his boat. He had to fight her tendency to dominate each scene. As Robert Jordan settled into the camp to await the proper time for blowing his bridge, he fell in love with Maria, a young Spanish girl who lived among the partisans.

"Now she looked him full in the face and smiled. Her teeth were white in her brown face and her skin and her eyes were the same golden tawny brown. She had high cheekbones, merry eyes and a straight mouth with full lips. Her hair was the golden brown of a grain field that has been burned dark in the sun but it was cut short all over her head so that it was little longer than the fur on a beaver pelt. She smiled in Robert Jordan's face and put her brown hand up and ran it over her head, flattening the hair which rose again as her hand passed. She has a beautiful face, Robert Jordan thought. She would be beautiful if they hadn't cropped her hair."

As he finished his first month's work on the novel it became clear that he could no longer work well in Key West. Pauline, accepting the coming end of their marriage, let Hemingway know that she intended to live her life in her home as she chose. That meant a full social schedule and frequent guests. If that disturbed Hemingway's routine, he was welcome to find other quarters. Hemingway took time to buy Pauline a new car, then boarded the *Pilar* and sailed to Havana, where Martha Gellhorn joined him in early April. The couple had spent enough time in hotels in Spain, she felt, and since their relationship gave promise of some permanence she began searching for a suitable home. She was taken by a twenty-one-acre estate in the village of San Francisco de Paula, less than twenty miles from Havana. The estate was called the Finca Vigía, the farm with a view. From the farm one could see the ocean and the streets of Havana. The house itself was in worse disrepair than had been his Key West home, and Hemingway refused to move in. He took his manuscript to sea aboard *Pilar*. While Hemingway fished, Martha hired craftsmen and servants, and upon Hemingway's return he moved into the Finca, as he called it, with Martha.

Although he told Maxwell Perkins that the new novel would be ready by late summer, he underestimated the size of the task he had set himself. The book was going to be much longer than anything else he'd ever attempted. By August he was three hundred typewritten pages into the book and had told less than half his story. At Pauline's request he attempted a last reconciliation at the Nordquists' L-Bar-T Ranch, where they had spent so many good summers. Their differences were too strong to overcome and Hemingway moved on to Sun Valley, Idaho, a resort area under development. He settled into a comfortable suite in the plush Sun Valley Lodge and called Martha Gellhorn to join him. The Sun Valley Lodge was owned by the Union Pacific Railroad, and in order to boost its reputation the lodge often offered accommodations to celebrities at substantial discounts. What was lost on the celebrities' bills would be made up for by the tourists attracted by their presence. Hemingway and Martha settled in for a long stay.

In Key West he had written in the mornings and fished in the afternoons. He followed the same routine in Idaho, substituting bird hunting for deep-sea fishing. He became close friends with many of the lodge's personnel, accompanying them on canoe or horseback hunting expeditions; saying a eulogy for the public relations director, who was killed in a hunting accident; becoming a favorite of the restaurant staff, who admired his enormous appetite. Hemingway worked well in Sun Valley, his production climbing with some frequency toward a thousand words a day. Often he wrote outside, dressed in the Western clothes he had come to admire, allowing the lodge's photographer to take some publicity pictures. In November Martha left on assignment to Finland for *Collier's*, but Hemingway remained in Sun Valley. His novel was going to be huge and he wanted to do nothing to break its smooth flow. He was beginning to understand the commitment a long novel imposes upon a writer, reconciling himself to a year's labor at the story of Robert Jordan and Maria. The results, he knew, would be worth the work.

Hemingway finally returned to Key West in December and spent Christmas alone in the house on Whitehead Street, packing the belongings he would take to Cuba. Early in 1940 Martha joined him at the Finca, aware that his break with Pauline was final, eager to undertake a full-time life with him. It was not an easy adjustment: Hemingway's discipline took him to his novel each morning, but his sense of fun kept him in Havana's bars until late each night. He took up cockfighting, seeing the sport in its own way as ritualistic and symbolic, raising fighting cocks at the Finca. The gang he assembled in Cuba did not delight Martha—Hemingway surrounded himself with exiled Spaniards for whom he bought drinks and told stories. When Martha questioned the professionalism of such heavy drinking, Hemingway laughed at her.

By March 1940 he had spent more than a year on the novel and a good amount of work remained to be done. War in Europe had erupted the previous fall, as he had predicted, and he remained concerned that America stay out of it. Bumby was nearly seventeen now, tall, broad-shouldered, and handsome, and Hemingway hated the thought of his son going to war. He had written thousands of words about war, thought of it constantly, proclaimed it to be the largest of the large themes for a writer, and despised with all his heart the way it wasted young men. He concentrated on his manuscript and attempted to shut out the tensions spreading across the world. The bridge that Robert Jordan was to blow was the only warfare Hemingway was immediately interested in.

The events in the book held him as though they were real— it was Hemingway's mission, it was his bridge. Almost as exciting was the sheer size of the story, and, for that matter, the manuscript. It was a big book in every way, filled with technical challenges that he'd worked hard to handle well, characters he'd shaped into life, military detail on which he considered himself an expert, miles of terrain made real because it was land he knew, a wonderful and sensual love story, and a sense throughout of an unavoidably tragic end. Hemingway knew what he had, and as summer approached he told people proudly that he was in the process of completing a great novel. He thought of Tolstoy and he thought of his novel as Tolstoyan—he felt it had the sweep and sensibility of *War and Peace,* of an epic. He spent hours looking through poems, plays, and the Bible for a title worthy of his work.

He finished the novel in July 1940. Some weeks earlier he had found his title while reading John Donne in the *Oxford Book of English Prose.* The passage that caught his attention read: "No man is an island, entire of itself; every man is a piece of the continent, a part of the main; if a clod be washed away by the sea, Europe is the less . . . any man's death diminishes me, because I am involved in mankind; and therefore never send to know for whom the bell tolls; it tolls for thee." Hemingway did not have to try hard to imagine the political reaction to his epigraph: on the eve of global war, people would say, Hemingway finally discovers a sense of belonging, of common purpose and community. They could say what they wanted and perhaps they were right. He called the novel *For Whom the Bell Tolls.*

Scribners rushed the book into production, delivering galley proofs of the text to Hemingway within a few weeks. They wanted the book on their fall list; it gave every indication of being a stupendous success. Excitement had been building for months, and the novel was the talk of New York even before it was finished. It seemed as though Hemingway's own sense of the book's value had spread throughout the reading public. As offers came in for various rights to the book, Hemingway and his publishers found even their largest expectations to be too small. The Book-of-the-Month Club contracted to print 100,000 copies for its members, the same number Scribners set for initial distribution to bookstores. People who read the manuscript and galleys said that no novel in years seemed so perfect for motion picture adaptation; dozens of copies were ordered by Hollywood producers. In October, when the film rights were sold, the deal shattered records. Hemingway received $100,000 for the film rights, along with ten cents for each copy sold in bookstores or by mail. Book-of-the-Month had already printed twice as many as originally planned and Scribners was well past 150,000 copies in print. Hemingway was rich. He celebrated in Sun Valley, where he hunted with Gary Cooper, the movie star he already thought of as Robert Jordan.

The critical reaction was not unanimous but was generally excellent. If no one was willing to compare Hemingway or his novel to Tolstoy and *War and Peace,* most felt that he had lived up to the promise shown in *A Farewell to Arms.* He had grown as a writer, and *For Whom the Bell Tolls* showed a more mature Hemingway, a writer who had his tendency to bully and breastbeat under control. The left-wing press claimed that Hemingway was exploiting the suffering of the Spanish Civil War, that Hemingway had no principles and had sold out their cause. Hemingway at first responded angrily to the charges, but later let them drop. He'd had his say about politics and political writers years before.

In November, slightly more than two weeks after his divorce from Pauline became final, he married Martha Gellhorn. He explained to the Catholic Church that Pauline's inability to bear further children rendered their marriage null; he was granted a dispensation to divorce her. After a brief honeymoon Hemingway used twelve thousand dollars of his money to purchase the Finca Vigía as a permanent home. He would become an expatriate again, living in Cuba on the banks of the Gulf Stream instead of in Paris near the Seine. As New Year's Day approached, he learned that Scott Fitzgerald had died of a heart attack in Hollywood while trying to complete a new novel.

With *For Whom the Bell Tolls* finished, Hemingway opened his eyes once more to the larger world. Europe was not the only continent under siege: totalitarianism was on the march across the globe. *Collier's* assigned Martha to cover the war in China, and Hemingway accompanied her to the Orient. They sailed for Hawaii in early January, and made their way from there by liner and aircraft. Hemingway bragged in April that he had flown more than 18,000 miles. His mood on the trip alternated between his customary eagerness at the prospect of experiencing something new, and his increasingly customary boredom and petulance. This was Martha's assignment, he said; he was just along for the ride.

While in China, Hemingway visited the front along with Martha. He filed several stories about the Chinese and their valiant struggle against the Japanese. These stories were more concerned with military detail than with human interest, and Hemingway admitted that his creative well was not replenished by Eastern culture. It was too different, too far removed from the world he knew. He was pleased, however, to be interviewed by major magazines as a world-respected expert on military theory and technology. By May Martha had left Hemingway behind as she pursued stories. They planned to reunite in New York later in the year and celebrate Hemingway's receipt of the Pulitzer prize in fiction. *For Whom the Bell Tolls* was the most talked-about novel of the year, the most widely respected. No one doubted that Hemingway would win the Pulitzer.

He did, by a unanimous vote of the Pulitzer board while Hemingway was still overseas. The board's chairman, however, held veto power and exercised it. It was his opinion that *For Whom the Bell Tolls* was an unworthy book, even a filthy one. There would be no Pulitzer prize in fiction for 1940. To Hemingway it was another echo of the objections he'd received from genteel readers since he was a boy. The denial of the prize also seemed an index of the book's effectiveness: if he could still offend people so strongly then he must be telling the absolute truth. Only truth earned strong reactions.

By the first anniversary of its publication, *For Whom the Bell Tolls* had sold more than 500,000 copies. With royalties from *The Fifth Column*, which had performed adequately despite poor reviews, Hemingway found his income for 1940 approached $150,000. Unfortunately nearly two-thirds of that was taken by the Internal Revenue Service, leaving him fuming. He was careful to pay his full share of taxes, though, fearing a battle with bureaucracy that would sap his energy and keep him from writing. He wanted to produce another book quickly to cap the success of his long novel. He gave thought to a new collection of short stories, to his study of the marlin, to a simpler book about Cuban fishermen and marlin. On December 7 the world intruded once more, the Japanese attack on Pearl Harbor putting to rest his writing career, perhaps for the duration of the war. There was a war on; Hemingway would be there.

His dilemma was to find the proper level of participation in the conflict. Hemingway had no interest in serving as a correspondent again; he had grown tired of journalism and often mocked Martha's dedication to a profession he considered at best second-rate. He was a writer of fiction and a man of action. If he could not write fiction, he would find some real action. He cast about for an assignment that would call upon all of his areas of expertise. As it became clear that German U-boats were patrolling the Caribbean in search of convoys, Hemingway hatched a plan.

He would outfit *Pilar* as a sort of guerilla vessel equipped with heavy machine guns and explosives. With a handpicked crew, he would patrol the sea under pretense of being a fisherman or marine scientist, hoping to draw the attention of a Nazi submarine. When the sub surfaced and summoned the *Pilar* alongside, Hemingway and his crewmen would ready themselves in the boat's high flying bridge, gathering to toss grenades and a heavy bomb down the sub's hatches. His machine gunners could handle any Germans who appeared on deck. He applied to United States naval intelligence for special equipment and radios, and although the officers were skeptical, they granted his request and assigned a marine to the boat.

Hemingway set a heavy schedule of patrols, his crew consisting of the marine, Spanish exiles, aging jai alai players, and guests from the Finca. For weeks they sailed virtually around the clock, seeing no submarines, practicing their grenade proficiency on targets and trash tossed into the sea. Martha did not hide her disdain for Hemingway's plan, and stopped in Cuba only briefly between journalistic trips. When Patrick and Gregory joined Hemingway for his period of summer custody, he immediately enlisted the boys in his crew. Patrick was fourteen and Gregory ten, and the prospect of spending a summer hunting submarines with their Papa seemed too good to be true.

As they cruised the Caribbean, Hemingway's thoughts were on parenthood. His only writing that year had been the introduction to an anthology of war stories he'd edited. He wrote as a father whose eldest son, at least, would certainly see combat. So might Patrick and Gregory, as well, if his plan came together properly. Hemingway tried to train the boys well, should they see action, and tried also to share their interests. Patrick was fascinated by astronomy and at night they used a telescope Hemingway bought for him. Gregory was already proving to be the family's finest wing shot and won a live pigeon–shooting contest at a Cuban sportsmen's club. Hemingway laughed along with Gregory at the newspapers' wildly exaggerated account of the boy's victory, but cautioned him firmly when he seemed to be growing too boastful. Both boys developed crushes on Martha, and learned to watch their father for the onset of a dark mood. When he was happy there was no finer father than Papa, and they often joined him for a ritual Bloody Mary at breakfast.

They saw no subs. The cover story of scientific research began to appeal as a means of alleviating the boredom of the empty sea, and they caught, preserved, and catalogued a variety of specimens, including a baby sailfish smaller than Hemingway's hand. They scanned the horizon constantly and listened to Hemingway curse the inaccuracy of navigational charts when *Pilar* ran aground. They lobbed grenades at slow-swimming turtles, caught marlin, made a base of an island barely a hundred yards in diameter, lived as pirates. Despite the training he gave, Hemingway did not plan to involve the boys in actual combat. He read to them and talked about books, was careful to speak well of their mother, and helped them raise a pig on the small island: it would make a fine barbecue. They laughed for days at the pig's escape, their final glimpse of it as a small dot on the horizon, swimming out to sea.

When they received word of a suspected German ammunition cache in the tunnels of a deserted island, Hemingway revved the *Pilar*'s engines and raced to the location. The tunnels were too small for adults and he sent Patrick and Gregory through them, warning them to retreat at the first sign of danger. The boys found no weapons but did retrieve several German beer bottles, their elation turning to disappointment when their father told them the bottles were pre-war, probably refuse from a picnic.

On days when the fishing was poor, Hemingway allowed his sons to spearfish along reefs. Gregory had caught several fish one afternoon and attached them to his belt, unaware that their blood was attracting sharks. Hemingway spotted the shark fins cutting the water, shouted to Gregory to abandon his fish, and dove off the side of the *Pilar*. Neither boy had ever seen anyone swim so fast as their father, who grabbed Gregory and pulled him through the water back to the boat.

The summer drew to a close. At last Hemingway set his course for Havana, where the boys would be sent on to Pauline. They stopped to help a Cuban fishing boat and joined a loud late-night celebration of a good catch. The next morning, slightly hung over as they made for home, they spotted a sub-marine near the horizon. Hemingway opened the *Pilar* full throttle, but the submarine was faster, and for what seemed like hours it pulled away and finally disappeared. Hemingway gathered his youngest sons close, sharing an indelible memory. Soon they were in Havana and the adventurous summer was over.

Hemingway continued his patrols into the fall, though not so frequently and with less pretense of naval discipline. He grew a full beard and ceased bathing. When Martha returned from an assignment she often found the Finca in chaos, the most com-mon housekeeping duties having been neglected for weeks. Hemingway's drinking had grown worse and he often poured his first Scotch well before noon. He was doing no writing. Martha's mockery of his patrols grew into open contempt: he was wasting his talent, and worse, he was contributing nothing to the war effort. Most nights he returned drunk and once he slapped her. Her response was to abandon him along the road to the Finca. She had no use for his bluster; she wanted to see his work. Hemingway continued to smile and boast that Papa knew more about war and writing than anyone. He had plenty left to write, he said, but his involvement in the war made it impossible to get to work. Martha's absences grew longer and longer.

By 1944 Hemingway was preparing to go to Europe. He'd waited, he said, until the Allies were on the offensive, until there was a real war to see. He was ready to go on the offensive himself after two years in the Caribbean without facing enemy fire. He was black from the sun with a beard that spread like a fan, showing generous growths of gray. Hemingway's forty-fifth birthday would come in July and he hoped to celebrate it on French soil. An invasion of Europe was looming sometime in the coming year and Hemingway intended to be a part of it. He flew across the Atlantic in mid-May, having abandoned his grimy and torn island clothes. Serving as a correspondent for *Collier's,* Hemingway wore a neat uniform that stretched taut over his greatly increased girth. He was purely Papa now, though, and slapped his full belly often, proclaiming its size a tribute to his gusto.

Martha was at sea, traveling with a convoy, and although they planned a London reunion, Hemingway knew that his third marriage was essentially over. He and Martha were both intensely competitive, but her sense of fair play did not match his. Hemingway blamed his wife, a good writer herself, for not understanding the nature and needs of a great writer. Settling into London's fashionable Dorchester Hotel, Hemingway considered himself a single man at war. He visited his brother Leicester, who was assigned to London, grew acquainted with Allied officers, and talked with other correspondents. He found himself increasingly interested in a tiny journalist named Mary Welsh. She was another good writer, a blonde from Minnesota, who came barely to Hemingway's chest. She was married, and attempted to cool the advances Hemingway sought to make. The war inspired him, he said, and he wrote poems to her, waging a campaign of his own.

In late May, after an evening of heavy drinking, Hemingway was badly injured when the jeep in which he rode crashed into a water tower. Hemingway's head went through the windshield, giving him a bad concussion and cutting him even more deeply than had the skylight accident years before. He took fifty-seven stitches but angrily resisted the doctors' orders confining him to bed. The invasion was imminent and he would not miss it. He was, he argued, a doctor's son who understood medicine. The doctors did not understand Hemingway's recuperative powers, and he was out of bed before the end of his month. The doctors' prohibition of alcohol struck him as equally unsound: a bandaged head would not keep him from putting his belly to a bar. He bought drinks and tried to learn the details of the invasion.

It came the night of June 5. Hemingway boarded a transport craft alongside thousands of GIs. Their destination was the coast of Normandy, the American landing site known as Omaha Beach. Although Hemingway was still in great pain and could move only slowly, he made his presence known in the transport's bridge and later in the landing craft making its way under heavy fire to the shore. Hemingway asked questions constantly, and offered advice and encouragement to those who would attempt to storm the beach. His injuries forced him to remain in the landing craft and return to the ships waiting offshore. He knew that Martha had landed and pressed inland along with the troops, and he was impatient to place himself more centrally in the action.

Hemingway was attracted to the Royal Air Force, as RAF pilots displayed a quiet courage that he much admired and wished to emulate. Despite constant headaches he attached himself to an RAF Wing whose mission was to shoot down V-1 buzz bombs before the German rockets fell on London. He strapped himself into the navigator's chair for the night missions, urging the flyers to turn and roll their craft sharply, laughing loudly as they pursued the missiles, announcing his fearlessness when anti-aircraft shells exploded around them. The pilots found Hemingway good company, but they were also professional British soldiers, who along with their fellows had seen nearly five years of brutal, wearying warfare. Hemingway's delight rang hollow in their ears.

War in the air was a fascinating experience, Hemingway admitted, but he was a ground soldier, a guerilla expert. Shortly after a forty-fifth birthday celebration—held in Normandy, as he had promised himself—Hemingway was assigned as correspondent accompanying the American 4th Infantry Division on its drive into France. He grew close to Colonel Charles Lanham and covered the advance of Lanham's 22nd Regiment. When the pace of the attack did not suit him, Hemingway took to riding ahead of the column, scouting the terrain, performing unauthorized reconnaissance missions. He rode in a captured Mercedes or in the sidecar of a motorcycle and boasted of the bravery of his drivers. Under German machine gun and tank fire, the motorcycle flipped, tossing Hemingway hard against a boulder. He escaped the Germans but for days he was bothered by blood in his urine from a blow to his kidneys and by double vision resulting from once more striking his head.

Despite the fierce German resistance, the Americans were moving steadily toward Paris. Hemingway's forward missions grew longer and ranged deeper into enemy territory. Although officially attached to the army and bound by the rules governing war correspondents' noncombatant status, Hemingway set his own agenda and made his own orders. The flyer's beard and uniform were gone now, and he dressed in fatigues, binoculars hung around his neck, canteens that were reliably reported to contain brandy and gin on each hip. Partisans and resistance fighters flocked to serve in his band of irregulars. All called him Papa and expressed their awe at his understanding of military operations. He organized the guerillas along his own line of command, mapped strategy, issued orders, behaved as a commander in the field should behave. Hemingway studied the maps carefully, keeping track of his group's position, the Germans', the army's. Allied command had assigned the task of entering Paris to a French division. Hemingway thought it would be possible to get there first.

By late August Paris was in sight. Hemingway pressed ahead, using his fluent French when asking directions, speaking German when interrogating his prisoners, leading his troops in songs he'd taught Bumby years before. The Nazis still occupied Paris when Hemingway and his crew rolled into the city on August 25, 1944. French tanks and infantry arrived simultaneously and Hemingway left the enemy to them—his goal was the liberation of the bar at the Ritz Hotel. He secured his objective with only minor fighting, and by late afternoon the champagne was flowing freely. Hemingway's largest grin flashed constantly as his troops, the men and women of Paris, and old friends who had remained in the city throughout the war came to the Ritz and clustered close, awestruck. Papa was the most magnificent soldier of all.

The army took a less admiring view of his exploits, and in October summoned Hemingway to headquarters to face charges that during his race for Paris he had violated the code of conduct required of correspondents. The questioning lasted an entire day, but Hemingway had prepared his answers carefully and called upon influential character witnesses. He was exonerated of all charges, and as the war entered its final winter Hemingway pressed on toward Germany. At the same time he pressed ahead with his courtship of Mary Welsh. Finding her resistance less stiff than the Nazis', Hemingway was unstoppable. He proposed marriage. His life with Martha Gellhorn was over, he said, and all he wanted after the war was to undertake a productive and happy life with Mary by his side. He called her "Pickle" and showered her with presents, poems, and pronouncements. He made it clear that he thought her marriage a joke, and one evening made his point dramatically. He locked himself in a hotel bathroom with a photograph of Mary's husband, set it up as a target on top of a toilet, and opened fire with his pistol, destroying the photograph and the plumbing, flooding the rooms below.

Her love outweighed her reservations, and Mary agreed to come to Cuba after the war. Hemingway accompanied American forces deep into Germany, proving his courage again and again, but by March 1945 he was ready to return to his Finca. He had seen enough; he had done enough. His war was over and he had writing to do.

FOURTEEN

CHAMPION

ERNEST HEMINGWAY'S DIVORCE from Martha Gellhorn became final on December 21, 1945. Three months later Hemingway married Mary Welsh. She had been with him in Cuba on and off since the previous spring, the two of them growing closer, Hemingway miserable when Mary was absent. The summer of 1945 had been a season of reunion, with Hemingway's sons joining them for long cruises on the *Pilar*, helping with lessons in marlin fishing and bird hunting for Mary. It was especially fine to have Bumby with them. He was a man now, Jack Hemingway, and he had served in the war as an operative for the Office of Strategic Services, parachuting behind enemy lines. He had been wounded and captured by the Germans, had escaped, and had been recaptured. Along the way, he had met one German officer from Schruns who remembered him as an infant and recalled his handsome young parents. Jack Hemingway had a lot of his father in him, and had embarked on his mission with his fly rod strapped to the barrel of his machine pistol. Now he was home, his health recovered, and Hemingway, greatly impressed, could hardly take his eyes off his son.

For more than half a year, Hemingway and Mary worked to get the Finca back in shape after the years of its owner's absence. They walked together over the grounds, learning the names of the hundreds of tropical flowers and plants that colored the countryside, supervised the construction of quarters for the dozens of cats Hemingway gave a home to, and planned improvements to the *Pilar* to make her an even better fishing machine. They spent time getting Hemingway in shape as well. He continued to suffer bad headaches as a result of his automobile crashes, and a Cuban physician strongly advised him to stop drinking. He was forty-six years old and could no longer treat his body as invincible: its vulnerability was clear from its many scars. He attempted to take the doctor's advice, cutting back on his consumption of alcohol, watching his weight and diet, toughening himself up in preparation for long hours at his desk once more. The war had provided Hemingway with a great variety of experiences, and he wanted to put them to use on paper, in fiction.

It was not the war, however, to which he turned when he resumed his writing career. He cast his mind back to the 1920s and began a novel about a writer and his wife in France. The book was called *The Garden of Eden,* and in it Hemingway sought to come to terms with his characters' sexuality, examining their ambiguous attachment to gender: in some scenes the man pretended to be a woman, the woman a man. It was a complex theme, easily as difficult as courage or war, and Hemingway worked hard on the book throughout 1946, passing the 1,000-page mark in his manuscript by his forty-seventh birthday. He wanted to return to fiction with a big book, bigger even than *For Whom the Bell Tolls*—a book that looked more deeply into human psychology, that broke new stylistic ground, that showed his ability to write well on subjects not usually associated with the Hemingway name. *The Garden of Eden,* he felt, would be his most ambitious work.

His birthday in July 1946 was a double celebration: Mary was pregnant. Hemingway, after years of calling every woman he knew "daughter," wanted a daughter of his own, and the prospect of parenthood delighted him enormously. As a reward for the hard work on a new novel, and a reward as well for the new life they had begun, Hemingway and Mary took a hunting holiday in Wyoming during which Mary collapsed. Her pregnancy was ectopic, the egg fertilized in a fallopian tube rather than in the womb, and although Hemingway rushed her to a hospital her critical condition quickly deteriorated. The doctors on call advised him that his wife was dying and urged him to make his farewells to her. Hemingway would have none of it. He was a doctor's son and had studied medicine all his life. He dressed himself quickly in a surgeon's gown and began snapping orders at the hospital staff, instructing them to find an intact vein and begin giving Mary transfusions of plasma and blood. The treatment worked, some said miraculously, and within a month Hemingway and Mary were in Sun Valley, Hemingway hunting while Mary continued to improve.

Although he continued to work on *The Garden of Eden* during 1947, Hemingway's dissatisfaction with the novel increased. It would require a great deal of rewriting before it was ready for publication, and the manuscript continued to grow past the thousand-page mark. He was eager to publish another novel—nearly a decade had passed since the triumph of *For Whom the Bell Tolls*—but it became clear that *The Garden of Eden*, which had already taken nearly two years of his life, would require at least that many more. Hemingway's income was not dependent upon a new novel, but his professional pride was. "The Short Happy Life of Francis Macomber," "The Killers," and other Hemingway short stories were much in demand in Hollywood, earning nearly as much apiece as had *For Whom the Bell Tolls.* The money was nice, but it brought with it tax problems and worries. They were worries he could live with, though, if he were publishing again. Late in 1948 he decided to get away from his desk, to take Mary on a trip to Italy where, as he approached his fiftieth birthday, he might regain some perspective and rejuvenate his creative powers.

Shortly before Christmas he met a young Italian girl, Adriana Ivancich. Hemingway was near the close of the first half-century of his life. Adriana was not quite nineteen, and her youth and beauty became for him a romantic obsession. He hovered close to her, fascinated by her eyes, her skin, her dark hair, praising her insights as wise beyond her years, sharing with her his own wisdom, never behaving in any way as other than a gentleman, paying no formal court but showing the courtly manner and grace of an older suitor. Mary seemed to understand, and said nothing. Her husband was happy, the flirtation was ultimately harmless, and best of all Hemingway was writing again. He began what he thought of as a short story, set in Italy, but it soon became obvious that he was actually at work on a novel. The work continued during the voyage back to Cuba, and picked up speed once Hemingway was back in the Finca.

The novel told the story of Colonel Robert Cantwell of the United States Army, stationed in Italy after the Second World War. Cantwell is fifty, as was his creator, infatuated with Renata, a nineteen-year-old Italian girl. In the novel the romance is erotic, gently so, as though Hemingway wrote of the relationship he might have enjoyed with Adriana Ivancich. But the new novel was more than just wish fulfillment. Colonel Cantwell is dying, his heart deteriorating, and Hemingway's novel was filled with a sense of melancholy, a dread of death but at the same time a deep fascination with it. Where he had found difficulty in writing of the young lovers in *The Garden of Eden*, their whole lives before them, he now wrote easily of the aging officer and his young love, of what they shared and feared.

"She kissed him kind, and hard, and desperately, and the Colonel could not think about any fights or any picturesque or strange incidents. He only thought of her and how she felt and how close life comes to death when there is ecstasy. And what the hell is ecstasy and what's ecstasy's rank and serial number? And how does her black sweater feel. And who made all her smoothness and delight and the strange pride and sacrifice and wisdom of a child? Yes, ecstasy is what you might have had and instead you draw sleep's other brother.

"Death is a lot of shit, he thought. It comes to you in small fragments that hardly show where it has entered. It comes, sometimes, atrociously. It can come from unboiled water; an unpulled-up mosquito boot, or it can come with the great, white-hot, clanging roar we have lived with. . . .

"It comes in bed to most people, I know, like love's opposite number."

He interrupted work on the new novel only for his birthday, putting to sea in the *Pilar* with friends and a case of champagne. The holiday did not last long, however, and he was back at his desk, alternating work on the new book with letters in which he said the novel was as good as Shakespeare. He thought it the best work he had ever done, and for the time called the book *A New Slain Knight,* a title that had intrigued him since the 1920s. It did not perfectly fit the book, however, and he at last selected as his title *Across the River and into the Trees,* a phrase based on Confederate General Stonewall Jackson's last words. Hemingway dedicated the novel to Mary; it was published in September 1950.

The literary world proclaimed the book a complete disaster, a catastrophe, proof that during the eleven years since *For Whom the Bell Tolls* Hemingway's talent had died. The passages about love and death with which the novel was riddled seemed amateurish and out of control. Some critics thought the book was unconscious parody, as though Hemingway, writing of even the smallest details of daily life as being done "truly" or "perfectly" or "awfully well," was making fun of his lifelong concern for accuracy and precision. Some said that Cantwell was a cartoon version of Hemingway, a thin character who mirrored his creator's lack of depth. Only novelist John O'Hara, writing in the *New York Times,* called it a great book, and said that Hemingway was the greatest writer since Shakespeare. That statement angered Hemingway nearly as much as the bad reviews—he felt O'Hara was being sycophantic, attempting to curry favor by saying what Hemingway wanted said. *Across the River and into the Trees* sold well, but its critical reception burned inside Hemingway. He became determined to prove the critics wrong, to show the world that he still knew more about writing than anyone alive.

Although from time to time he picked up work on *The Garden of Eden,* his primary concern in the early 1950s was a long novel based in part on his experiences in the Second World War. The project began as a trilogy, with separate novels planned to deal with the war at sea, the war on land, and the war in the air. Gradually the plan evolved into a single long novel about the sea. The novel would have three parts: *The Sea When Young, The Sea When Absent,* and *The Sea in Being.* Throughout 1950 he worked on the book, each section a novel in itself, spending most of his time on *The Sea When Absent,* telling the story of a painter, Thomas Hudson, and his life in the Caribbean. The work pleased Hemingway and his confidence grew daily. When William Faulkner was awarded the Nobel Prize in literature, Hemingway felt sufficiently calm to be magnanimous. He sent Faulkner a congratulatory telegram, telling friends that Faulkner had earned the prize, dismissing the many derogatory comments he had made about Faulkner over the years.

His fascination with Adriana Ivancich was undiminished, and he invited Adriana and her mother to the Finca for Christmas 1950. As always when near Adriana, Hemingway's spirits soared, and he played the attentive, eager host. He bragged that she was the best thing that ever happened to his work, and rose with the dawn to reach his desk by first light each morning. His novel of the sea had grown more complex, an idyllic section with Thomas Hudson and his sons to be followed by a section with Hudson at sea, using his fishing boat to hunt down German submarines. The sea novel would be wonderful, not only embracing everything Hemingway knew about the ocean, but also having wonderful characters and exciting scenes of combat. It would prove, he felt, that in his maturity he could use his talent to come to terms with complex themes, but he also knew that the sea, like death, was simple as well as complex. As 1951 began he undertook the last section of the novel, *The Sea in Being*, which would be shorter than the other sections and would have no characters in common with them. *The Sea in Being* would be a simple story, as simple as anything Hemingway had ever written, and yet it too would have all of the sea and all of courage in it. The story had been on his mind since his first days in Key West, more than two decades earlier, and he had tried to write it before. Now, happily married to Mary, and happily in love with Adriana, Hemingway began to tell the story of a Cuban marlin fisherman named Santiago and his heroic battle with a marlin, and then with the sharks that would deny him his prize.

"He was an old man who fished alone in a skiff in the Gulf Stream and he had gone eighty-four days now without taking a fish. In the first forty days a boy had been with him. But after forty days without a fish the boy's parents had told him that the old man was now definitely and finally *salao*, which is the worst form of unlucky, and the boy had gone at their orders in another boat which caught three good fish the first week. It made the boy sad to see the old man come in each day with his skiff empty and he always went down to help him carry either the coiled lines or the gaff and harpoon and the sail that was furled around the mast. The sail was patched with flour sacks and, furled, it looked like the flag of permanent defeat."

Every lesson Hemingway had learned about writing, every theory he had developed, every discipline in which he believed, was at work as he fashioned the story of Santiago the fisherman. He stripped his prose more clean than he had in years, making each word contribute to the story, guarding against the intrusion of the author's personality, wanting only to tell his story with absolute ease, clarity, and truth. Adriana's presence, he felt, had helped him get started, but her departure early in 1951 could not stop him. It seemed that the story developed a momentum of its own, in a way that no other piece he had ever written had done, and he was as happy as a child when he showed sections of the manuscript to Mary and others. They were in agreement, as anyone who read the book would be: Hemingway was embarked upon a masterpiece. With simple, declarative sentences, he followed Santiago to sea, to the hooking of a marlin.

"The line rose slowly and steadily and then the surface of the ocean bulged ahead of the boat and the fish came out. He came out unendingly and water poured from his sides. He was bright in the sun and his head and back were dark purple and in the sun the stripes on his sides showed wide and a light lavender. His sword was as long as a baseball bat and tapered like a rapier and he rose his full length from the water and then reentered it, smoothly, like a diver and the old man saw the great scythe-blade of his tail go under and the line commenced to race out."

Everything Hemingway knew about marlin—all the knowledge gathered for the unwritten history of the great fish—went into the narrative. The solitary struggle against the pull of the marlin, the expanse of the sea, the final victory over the fish undone when sharks attack the marlin's body: Hemingway's Santiago came to terms with each of these struggles, refusing to surrender no matter how deeply he wished he could. "'But man is not made for defeat,' he said. 'A man can be destroyed but not defeated.'"

Hemingway finished the story in February. Barely one hundred pages long, it would serve as a perfect coda, or epilogue, to his much larger narrative of Thomas Hudson. He was now calling that book *The Island and the Stream,* and returned to it immediately upon completing the story of Santiago. He enjoyed writing the early sections of the Thomas Hudson book, recreating Bimini as he had known it in the 1930s, putting Bumby, Patrick, and Gregory in the book as Hudson's sons. The novel began well, but it did not satisfy Hemingway. It would be measured, he knew, against its coda, that perfect short novel, and it would not pass comparison. In writing of Santiago he had put on paper one man's struggle to maintain his dignity against natural adversaries, and against his own impulse to surrender. Thomas Hudson's world was more artificial, more complex. Truths were not so self-evident in that story, and Hemingway began to think of publishing the novella separately.

His mind was made up early in 1952 when *Life* magazine agreed to publish *The Old Man and the Sea,* as Hemingway called the story, in a single issue. Scribners would follow magazine publication with a hardcover edition, whose cover would be drawn by Adriana Ivancich. The Book-of-the-Month Club made the novella a main selection. Everyone agreed that the book would prove popular, but when the September 1, 1952, issue of *Life* appeared, its success was stunning. More than five million copies of the magazine were sold in its first two days on sale. People who read the novella in the magazine wept openly at its beauty, and purchased hardcover copies to keep and give away; Scribners sold more than fifty thousand copies during the first few days the book was available. Hemingway and his story became the subject of sermons and editorials, but these were filled with praise for the taste and dignity of his story, rather than the condemnations of brutality that he recalled from earlier in his career. Strangers telephoned the Finca to tell Hemingway his work had changed their lives. Hemingway received more than five hundred letters a week, personal messages of acclaim and gratitude. *The Old Man and the Sea* was a story for everyone, and it held a power and a beauty that could change people's lives. Hemingway accepted the response gracefully, and smiled knowingly as he read reviews in which critics reversed their opinion of him. For a time he was almost modest about the book, pausing only occasionally—usually after a few drinks—to dare anyone to say that William Faulkner could have done as well as Ernest Hemingway. No one took him up on the dare.

For all the triumph, his thoughts remained filled with death. Maxwell Perkins had been gone for five years, dying before his star writer achieved his greatest success. In June 1951, Grace Hall Hemingway died at seventy-nine. Hemingway did not object when a nearby church tolled a bell in his mother's honor, but he also did not attend her funeral. He had said many times that Grace ruined his father's life, and he would let that comment stand as her epitaph. He was less prepared, however, for Pauline's death, at fifty-six, early in October 1951. She had gone to San Francisco to help Gregory with some legal difficulties, and for a time Hemingway blamed the boy for Pauline's death. By late 1952, as the tumult over *The Old Man and the Sea* began to settle, Hemingway's thoughts were filled with his own mortality.

Not that it had ever been far from his mind. When writing *The Old Man and the Sea*, in fact, he had thought at one point to kill Santiago, to show the old man as unable to survive the enormous challenges put before him. That thought had passed and Hemingway felt that his current preoccupation with death would pass as well. As 1953 began, he was making preparations for another safari at last. Twenty years had passed since his previous trip to Africa, and he remembered well the trophies and stories that expedition yielded. All he needed now to take his mind off his blood pressure was the sight of the African hills, a solid rifle in his hands, and good companions by his side. He struck a deal to write of the safari for *Look* magazine, and arranged to travel once more with Philip Percival, who, like Hemingway, had gray hair now. An added delight on the trip would be the opportunity to visit Patrick Hemingway, who shared his father's love of Africa, and who owned a 3,000-acre farm in Tanganyika.

Hemingway and Mary stopped first in Spain for the bullfights in Pamplona. By late August they were encamped with Philip Percival, Hemingway killing a rhinoceros, several zebra, a lion, and a leopard in the first weeks of the safari. He experienced occasional difficulty with his vision, and its effect on his aim annoyed him. The fact of Africa, though, its presence all around him, was the best medicine in the world. His weight and his blood pressure dropped; his stamina increased. By January 1954, he felt as though he were in his twenties again: he was walking miles with Mary, shooting well, flirting with young African girls. He looked forward to flying with Mary on a sightseeing trip to Uganda.

Africa was as breathtaking from the air as from the ground. For three days Hemingway, Mary, and their pilot soared above great waterfalls and lakes, photographing huge herds of animals, swooping low over tribesmen in canoes. They were so taken with Murchison Falls that they asked the pilot to loop over the white water once more, to give them a better view. The pilot did as requested, but was startled by a flight of birds, dipped too low and brushed against a telegraph wire, damaging both the propeller and the tail of his aircraft. He could not hold altitude and the plane responded only sluggishly to his controls. The pilot managed to clear the hills beside the waterfall, and came down hard three miles from the river. Hemingway's shoulder was sprained by the crash, and Mary was in shock for a time, but their pilot was well and all were aware of how much more serious the accident could have been. In the morning they were found by a party of tourists who carried them by boat back to civilization.

Hemingway was amused upon his return to find that during the night they were missing he had been reported dead. A search was under way. Hemingway made clear that he was all right, and arranged for another airplane to fly him and Mary to Entebbe, where they could rest in comfort. They boarded the new airplane late in the afternoon, strapped in for the flight, and had not been airborne more than a few moments when the plane crashed and caught fire. Mary escaped through a window, but Hemingway used his head to butt open a door. They stepped back from the burning fuselage, Mary limping badly, Hemingway watching the fire intently. In his escape he had split his skull, losing not only blood but also serum from inside his head. He was weak, his vision was cloudy and sometimes double, but he insisted to Mary and the press that he was fine, that his luck continued to protect him.

By the time they reached Entebbe—by automobile—

Hemingway had summoned the strength to pose for the press. He knew how badly he was hurt—his left eye was blind, his right ear deaf, his face and hands burned—but he knew also that the eyes of the world were on him. Reports of his death had traveled quickly, and international newspapers in Entebbe carried his name in large letters above long columns of obituary. There had been no time for new editions of the newspapers to appear with corrected reports, but word had reached his friends and fans, and the Entebbe telegraph office was kept busy accepting cables of good wishes and happiness. Hemingway took pleasure in the cables, but what delighted him most were the many death notices in the papers, and the accompanying thoughts on his passing collected from writers, statesmen, and celebrities throughout the world. He wanted to know who had said what of him, who had told the truth and who lied, how his measure had been taken.

Despite his injuries Hemingway was not ready to give up the expedition. A medical examination revealed serious internal problems, including a crushed vertebra and ruptured liver, but Hemingway remained in bed only a few weeks. After rushing through a piece for *Look*—dictated against his own sense of his best working habits—he joined Patrick on the coast, where he had chartered a fishing boat. He did not fish, but to prove his health he hurried to join the battle against a wildfire, only to grow dizzy and collapse into the flames, burning himself badly over much of his body. By March he was in Europe once more with Mary, first to visit Adriana, then taking a driving tour of the Spanish countryside in which he had set *For Whom the Bell Tolls*. Back in Cuba at last, he passed his fifty-fifth birthday quietly, recuperating at the Finca with his wife, his fishing boat, his cats, and his collection of clippings containing stories of his own death.

FIFTEEN

END

THE NOBEL PRIZE FOR literature was awarded to Ernest Hemingway on October 28, 1954. His reactions were mixed. The award carried with it $35,000, which he welcomed, but he could live without the publicity it generated. Hemingway bragged briefly of his intention to turn down the award, perhaps with an obscene statement, but in the end gave a relaxed and gracious interview in which he cited writers who he admired but who had never won the prize. He worried that the turmoil and celebration would affect his writing, which he was attempting to bring once more under control. He disliked the image of himself as a distinguished elder statesman of American literature. Most of all he was annoyed by the statement from the Nobel Prize committee that made the award. There could be no mistaking the fact that *The Old Man and the Sea* had worked its magic on the committee. They saw in the novella all of the virtues their prize was to uphold: decency, respect for the human spirit, the dignity of man. Those virtues were absent in Hemingway's earlier work, which the committee called callous and brutal, using two words that had been used in accusations against Hemingway since his first publication. *Time* prepared another cover story on Hemingway, who did not go to Sweden to accept the Nobel Prize. He did not feel well enough to attend: the injuries sustained in the airplane crashes continued to bother him, and he continued to wrestle with his writing.

He was working on another African book, which he thought at first might become a novel. It settled only gradually into its final form, a narrative of his safari with Mary not unlike *Green Hills of Africa*. Although his back gave him constant pain, Hemingway kept his discipline, which consisted of early hours and hard work with a pencil. The pages piled up, passing four hundred by summer 1955, but he was unhappy with them. On some pages and on some days he wrote wonderfully, getting down everything he recalled in just the right words and the right order. On other days, sentences gave him endless difficulty. He put the African story aside and switched to short stories, which sold easily but seemed far below his own standards. He returned to the African book, pushing it past seven hundred pages before the end of the year.

A film version of *The Old Man and the Sea* was being made, with Hemingway hired to catch marlin from the *Pilar* while cameras rolled. None of the Gulf Stream marlin were large enough to pass for Santiago's great fish, and the film company flew Hemingway to the coast of Peru, off which larger marlin, rumor said, were to be found. The trip yielded no fish suitable for the film, and the producers ultimately used an artificial marlin, courtesy of their special effects department. Hemingway became friends with Spencer Tracy, who was portraying Santiago, but had otherwise no use for the people of Hollywood. Their presence bothered him; their attitude toward his work disgusted him. The only thing he liked was their money, and even most of that was quickly devoured by the Internal Revenue Service. He wanted more than anything to go on safari again, but his doctors and Mary forbade it, forcing him to settle for a long trip to Europe. They attended the bullfights in Spain, and then Hemingway and Mary went to Paris.

They spent the 1956 Christmas holidays at the Ritz, relaxing in rooms where Hemingway had fought and drunk a dozen years earlier. From the hotel management he received the nicest Christmas present of all. While cleaning a basement, hotel employees had discovered two dilapidated trunks full of notebooks and manuscripts that Hemingway had stored at the Ritz after the publication of *The Sun Also Rises*. Hemingway had completely forgotten the manuscripts, and was stunned to have them, faded but still legible, before him. It was almost as good as finding the manuscripts that had been stolen from Hadley. Those were gone forever, though, and these were a treasure in themselves. He pored over them, letting them carry him back to his youth, to the sights and sounds of Paris as he had known it during the 1920s. By summer he had returned to Cuba, where the manuscripts served as a sort of catalyst for his creativity, the associations that rose in his memory from their words bringing forth new words now, as he began a book of sketches about Paris and his youth.

"Then there was the bad weather. It would come in one day when the fall was over. We would have to shut the windows in the night against the rain and the cold wind would strip the leaves from the trees in the Place Contrescarpe. The leaves lay sodden in the rain and the wind drove the rain against the big green autobus at the terminal and the Café des Amateurs was crowded and the windows misted over from the heat and the smoke inside."

He captured not only the sense of Paris, its seasons and its architecture, but also the people he'd known, who'd influenced him and helped him, friends who'd encouraged him as he learned to write. Most of them were dead by now, and Hemingway felt free to write as he pleased. He wrote of Scott Fitzgerald, "the way things were going, he was lucky to get any work done at all. Zelda did not encourage the people who were chasing her and she had nothing to do with them, she said. But it amused her and it made Scott jealous. . . . It destroyed his work, and she was more jealous of his work than anything." He related unfortunate incidents about Ezra Pound, Gertrude Stein, Ford Madox Ford, and others. His prose was as wonderful as ever, and if he showed little sympathy toward his subjects, he was equally harsh on himself. He recalled the sacrifices he'd forced upon Hadley and Bumby in the name of his art, and re-created his feelings, once the sacrifice began to pay off, on leaving Hadley.

"When I saw my wife again standing by the tracks as the train came in by the piled logs at the station, I wished I had died before I ever loved anyone but her. She was smiling, the sun on her lovely face tanned by the snow and sun, beautifully built, her hair red and gold in the sun, grown out all winter awkwardly and beautifully, and Mr. Bumby standing with her, blond and chunky and with winter cheeks. . . .

"I loved her and I loved no one else and we had a lovely magic time while we were alone. I worked well and we made great trips, and I thought we were invulnerable again, and it wasn't until we were out of the mountains in late spring that the other thing started again."

Hemingway completed the book of sketches in 1958, and by summer was attempting to get the book in shape for publication. When work went poorly on it he would shift to one of his three other large manuscripts, still working occasionally on *The Garden of Eden*, or his Thomas Hudson story *The Island and the Stream*, or his long African narrative. Many days the work did not go well at all. He was fifty-nine years old; he continued to have trouble with his eyes and back; his blood pressure climbed frighteningly high. Political difficulties also spoiled his concentration: the Batista government of Cuba was in the process of being overthrown by Fidel Castro's revolution, and although Hemingway had spent his entire life admiring guerilla fighters such as Castro's, he now worried about the Finca and about his safety. He felt that his years in Cuba at his beloved farmhouse were coming to an end, and early in 1959 purchased a home on the mainland, a lovely home on a hill above a river outside Ketchum, Idaho. It would be a place to go if Cuba became too dangerous.

The summer of 1959 would bring his sixtieth birthday and Hemingway intended to celebrate with a long trip to Spain for the bullfights. *Life* magazine asked him to cover the season for them, requesting 10,000 words of Hemingway's prose to accompany their photographs. Hemingway accepted the assignment happily. It would be an interesting season and no one could write of it better than he. Everything had to be exactly right, everyone had to follow his instructions. When Mary broke a toe, he accused her of attempting to spoil his summer. When she worked hard to make his sixtieth birthday celebration something special, Hemingway drank too much and became abusive and obscene toward her. No one understood the symbolism of the bullfight, he argued, no one understood its importance to him. Mary Hemingway, though, was as strong as Hemingway himself, and she did understand better than anyone how badly he'd been hurt and how many times he'd been hurt, and knew something of the toll his injuries had taken on his body and his mind. She stood by him.

By late fall he had returned to America and set to work on the bullfight piece for *Life*. The piece grew rapidly and he began to tell people that no one could even approach the bullfight in a few thousand words. By April 1960 his manuscript had passed the 100,000-word mark, with another month's work to go before it was finished. The editors at *Life* were shocked when they viewed the book which Hemingway called *The Dangerous Summer*. It was not simply that the work was far too long: the prose was weak and repetitive, the insights secondhand and poorly considered. It was a delicate editorial process, Hemingway's wrath risked at every suggested cut, but by summer a long excerpt had been prepared. Hemingway had lost confidence in the accuracy of the piece and flew to Spain for a final visit to check details and go over photographs. The trip was hectic and he was filled with tension, worrying about little things, unable to sleep, fearful of conspiracies. His moods went up and down without control. He hated the thought of returning to the United States, convinced that at last the Internal Revenue Service was going to indict and imprison him.

There was no question now of returning to Cuba. Mary took

an apartment in New York and Hemingway passed his sixty-first birthday there, worried about the Finca, about the *Pilar*, about his career and his dwindling powers. He resisted requests that he leave the apartment, convinced that the FBI had him under surveillance. Although the amounts earned for motion picture rights to his stories grew larger every year, he was certain that he was impoverished, that he and Mary would soon be begging for subsistence. He could not write, and if he did not have his profession, how could he expect to support a household? His blood pressure climbed; his kidneys bothered him. Near the end of 1960 Mary flew him to Rochester, Minnesota, where, to avoid publicity, she registered Hemingway under an assumed name at the Mayo Clinic.

He was kept under observation, undergoing tests and therapy, for nearly two months. To counter Hemingway's deep depression, the doctors put him through a regimen of electroshock treatments twice a week. At Christmas they allowed him to go target shooting, and he proved that his aim remained excellent. His spirits seemed to rise as well and as the New Year came he spoke of getting back to work. With Mary he watched the inauguration of John Kennedy, and sent the new President two telegrams of congratulation and Godspeed. He thought he recognized something in Kennedy, that understanding of courage that came from facing danger and pain. By late January the doctors released him and Mary took him home to Ketchum.

The first task facing Hemingway was the composition of a brief sentence requested to honor President Kennedy. His telegrams had come easily but he spent hours trying to write a simple declarative sentence, and finally collapsed in tears. He could no longer write, and abandoned the task. His sense of failure and fear mounted. He called Hadley and talked for a while, but she hardly recognized his voice. In April 1961, Mary caught him holding a shotgun and a suicide note. Only an hour of her calm, sensible, loving conversation prevented him from killing himself. She arranged for his immediate readmission to the Mayo Clinic. Hemingway attempted suicide twice more—once by trying to walk into the spinning propeller of an airplane—before reaching Rochester.

Hemingway remained in the clinic for several weeks, finally persuading his doctors that he was fine, that his suicide attempts had been a result of a temporary loss of his powers. Now he was ready to work again, he told them, and to do better work than he had ever done before. The doctors saw great improvement in his condition. When Mary was alone with her husband, though, she could tell that his behavior was an act for the doctors. When there were no doctors to overhear him, Hemingway's demons were unleashed. He'd lived too well, he'd become too famous, he'd written too many unpopular truths—now he would have to pay. The government was after him; the police were after him. Mary tried to convince the doctors to hold Hemingway in the hospital for his own good, but they were confident of their cure. Hemingway was released in late June, not long before he would turn sixty-two.

At the house in Ketchum, friends came to visit and were shocked by Hemingway's deterioration. He looked like a small old man, almost too frail to walk. His arms were as thin as sticks, his eyes empty and distant, his conversations filled with pauses that became silences. Mary had locked away all of his guns, and he had promised the doctors that he would not kill himself. On July 1 he managed to accompany her to a restaurant where he at first ate quietly and even drank a little wine. Soon, though, he began to speculate about the number of FBI agents in the restaurant, watching him. By the time they returned home he was calm once more, and went to bed quietly.

The next morning was Sunday, July 2, 1961. Hemingway rose before Mary, and while she slept he looked silently for the hiding place for the household keys. He found them and took a shotgun and shells from the storage room in the basement. He went to the foyer and loaded the shotgun. Years before, tall and strong, he'd talked of how it was possible to trip both triggers of a shotgun with a bare toe. Now he steadied the gun butt against the floor and rested his head against the barrels, and in the early morning light ended his life.

His funeral took place on July 5. Television cameras covered the burial of Ernest Hemingway, and friends and family came from across the world to pay their respects. At Mary's request the shotgun he'd used to kill himself was cut into pieces and buried somewhere else, in an unknown spot in the Idaho hills.

EPILOGUE
ERNEST HEMINGWAY TODAY

THAT HEMINGWAY'S DEATH WOULD be a major news story was, of course, already known. Among his estate a collection of yellowing obituaries offered prescient testimony to the celebrity value of Hemingway dead. This time the obituaries were accurate, and his suicide made headlines worldwide.

At first, the death was reported as an accident, but the truth soon surfaced. Suicide gave those who had for years fashioned careers out of speculations on Ernest Hemingway's psychology an entirely new field to work. Could they find the seeds of his suicide in the pages of his books? Second-guessing Hemingway's suicide became virtually a small industry unto itself, with theories and explanations for the suicide filling newspaper columns, magazine articles, and, later, entire books. The theories proved as various as their authors, but proved little. An explanation might best be obtained by paraphrasing Hemingway himself: he died, and then he was dead.

The work he had done during his lifetime remained alive, however, and as the gossip columnists and pseudo-psychologists wrestled with his corpse, the critics—Hemingway's old nemeses—wrestled with his literary corpus. What was Hemingway's position in American literature? Was he, as he had so often proclaimed, the best, the champion? Such questions are finally unanswerable, but a full-scale critical revision got quickly under way. During the 1960s and 1970s, the academic and literary communities relegated Ernest Hemingway and his work to lower and lower status. If they could not make a convincing case for labeling him a minor writer, many critics argued that he at least had not been a major writer.

Despite the prizes he'd been awarded, despite Hemingway's enormous popularity and the phenomenal success of *The Old Man and the Sea,* the critical consensus after Hemingway's death was that he had ultimately failed as an artist. Hemingway's work as a stylist had certainly exercised a revolution in prose, but he had never delivered the ambitious novel many expected. *For Whom the Bell Tolls* fell from favor, coming to be seen as a fantasy romance of heroism and doomed love. *To Have and Have Not* and *Across the River and into the Trees* were declared to be minor works, and flawed minor works at that. Even *The Old Man and the Sea* failed fully to survive the new critical scrutiny: the book was too simple, some critics said; it lacked the complexity necessary for an important work. Hemingway's nonfiction, the journalism and *Death in the Afternoon* and *Green Hills of Africa,* were viewed as interesting only in the ways in which they shed light on Ernest Hemingway's character and obsessions.

There was important work among Hemingway's books: *The Sun Also Rises, A Farewell to Arms,* and many of the short stories retained their power and beauty, the critical line went. But, the line went on, wasn't that really a rather small achievement? Certainly Hemingway had not left an artistic record on the order of that of William Faulkner, his old rival. Even Scott Fitzgerald, whose work at one time had been out of print, received a more admiring critical press during the 1960s and 1970s than did Ernest Hemingway.

How could Hemingway have fallen from grace so quickly? In part his decline can be seen as a measure of the times during which the revision occurred. The virtues Hemingway extolled in his work—courage, masculinity, grace under fire—seemed out of place to many in the 1960s. Bravery was old-fashioned, courage an anachronism in the shadow of nuclear weapons. What place could grace hold on a battlefield whose combatants were missiles, not men? War, in Hemingway's life and art the great consolidating experience, became the object of protest, soldiers the object of scorn.

As the women's movement gathered strength during the decades after Hemingway's death, his hairy-chested masculinity was denounced as foolish and even dangerous. Feminist writers attacked Hemingway's work with some frequency. Racist and anti-Semitic strains were found and denounced in his work. Even the hunting and fishing expeditions, so long seen as tests of courage and celebrations of the adventurous life, were now condemned as cruel, even perverse. Thanks to Hemingway and others like him, it was argued, many noble species came to be balanced on the edge of extinction.

But there is the critical community, and there is the reading public. Ernest Hemingway's work fell into academic disrepute, but readers never lost their admiration for Hemingway's achievement. His concerns—courage, dignity, clarity of thought and expression—proved themselves universal; the manifestations of his personality had interest without damaging the value of the work. Hemingway's books remained in print and sold well in hard and soft covers; films made of the books and stories attracted audiences; works unpublished at his death found eager readers when they came to be published.

Mary Hemingway proved herself an able and careful manager of her husband's literary estate. There was no rush to get Hemingway's unpublished works into print. The first of the books to be published posthumously was the collection of sketches of Paris and Hemingway's youth, which in 1964 was brought out by Scribners as *A Moveable Feast*. It received generally respectful reviews, although the cruelty that colored many of Hemingway's portraits bothered some.

In 1970 Mary Hemingway chose to publish one of Hemingway's novels. This was the large sea story on which he had worked, under several titles, at various times during the last fifteen years of his life. The story of Thomas Hudson, artist—a not heavily disguised portrait of Hemingway himself—was published by Scribners as *Islands in the Stream.* The novel made the best-seller lists immediately and, though flawed, earned respectable reviews. Hemingway had not considered the book finished, but, except for some unspecified cuts in the manuscript, the book was published as written. The last section of *Islands in the Stream* told the story of Hudson's use of his fishing boat in pursuit of Nazis, and was an exciting if somewhat confused and incredible adventure story. The first section of the book, though, dealt with Hudson's life in Bimini and the long summer visit of his three sons, and was a fine, moving, and in places very funny novella.

Two years later, Scribners collected the Nick Adams stories and added a good number of unpublished fragments about Nick, one of them, of some length, perhaps the beginning of a novel. *The Nick Adams Stories* put the stories for the first time into chronological order, but the arrangement did little to increase the stories' already high stature. The fragments were interesting, although generally undistinguished, and the book was not a great success with the critics or the public.

The Wild Years, published in 1962, and *By-Line: Ernest Hemingway,* which appeared in 1967, collected Hemingway's newspaper and magazine journalism. In the case of these two volumes, chronological order became a genuine contribution, making Hemingway's skills, limitations, and growth as a journalist, a writer, and a celebrity evident.

Some manuscripts still await publication. *The Garden of Eden,* by reputation the longest and most unusual of Hemingway's novels, remains unpublished, although rumors of its imminent appearance surface occasionally. Two sizable nonfiction books, *The Dangerous Summer*—the bullfight article commissioned by *Life* but too long and rambling for complete publication—and his book-length journal of the final African safari, are likely to be put into print in years to come. A very few short stories remain uncollected.

Although Ernest Hemingway maintained that he did not wish his correspondence ever to be published—and made a sort of legal provision against such publication—Mary Hemingway bravely and wisely countermanded his instructions and in 1981 brought out *Ernest Hemingway: Selected Letters, 1917–1961*. The book is nearly one thousand pages long and was assembled under the editorship of Dr. Carlos Baker, the best of Hemingway's many biographers. The letters are pure Hemingway: loud, brash, compassionate, learned, funny, obscene, insecure, provocative, contemptuous. It is good to have the letters in print, and reading them brings their author to life as fully as can a biography.

Hemingway's name remains in the public eye in other ways than through his books. Bumby—now known as Jack—frequently appears on television wielding a fly rod, catching—and releasing—large trout. His granddaughters are even more famous. Margaux is a model and actress, and Mariel Hemingway is an actress who seems likely to become a major motion picture star. Both women are striking, with broad, familiar Hemingway grins.

As the century moves toward its close, Hemingway's position is becoming more secure, his reputation once more on the rise. Ernest Hemingway worried about such things, but need not have been too much concerned finally with his popular recognition. A quarter of a century after his death, the name *Ernest Hemingway* remains in many minds synonymous with "American writer," and his influence on younger writers continues undiminished. It is interesting, if empty, to speculate upon what he would have made of this modern world of computers, ambisexuality, television, movie stars who were his granddaughters, biological engineering, space travel. Interesting but empty, because with his death Hemingway dealt himself out of confrontation with a world in transition. He had seen enough transitions in his lifetime, and he left his life only after capturing, in works that may live forever, his reactions to those changes, his life and his attitudes, his fears and bravery, and the fears and attitudes and lives of another, now gone, age.

ACKNOWLEDGMENTS AND REFERENCES

ERNEST HEMINGWAY'S RELATIONSHIP with the publishing community and with his publishers was so much a part of his life and this little book that it seems appropriate to begin this section with a nod toward my own. Herb Katz of M. Evans and Company asked for this biography, and Linda Cabasin, a wonderful editor, offered much encouragement and advice during its composition. Thanks are also due to Henry Morrison and to Leslie Owen of his office.

For important biographical material supplied at exactly the right times during my research, I want to extend my appreciation to Sam and Ginny Sparrow, to Pat McDaid, and to Les Butchart. Martha Ferrell and Alec Ferrell, my family, helped more than they know.

Ernest Hemingway's life is probably as well documented as that of any writer, and the biographical references upon which I most heavily leaned are divided into two sections:

WORKS BY HEMINGWAY'S FAMILY

At the Hemingways [sic]: *A Family Portrait,* by Marcelline Hemingway Sanford (Boston: Atlantic-Little, Brown, 1962), is a long and idyllic memoir by Hemingway's older sister. This book is far more sympathetic to Grace Hall Hemingway than was Ernest Hemingway.

Leicester Hemingway sought to create a career for himself as a novelist and journalist, and although he published several books, he never escaped from the shadow cast by his older brother. *My Brother, Ernest Hemingway* (New York: The World Publishing Company, 1962) tells the story of his relationship with his brother. Of particular interest are Leicester Hemingway's versions of many of the famous stories about his brother. Sadly, Leicester Hemingway committed suicide in 1982.

Ernie: Hemingway's Sister "Sunny" Remembers, by Madelaine Hemingway Miller (New York: Crown Publishers, Inc., 1975), delivers exactly what its title promises: the reminiscences of Sunny Hemingway and the story of the hero worship she felt for her older brother. This is a brief, sprightly, funny book that raises, as do both of the memoirs listed above, some questions of accuracy, but which is nonetheless enjoyable and entertaining.

Of Hemingway's sons, only Gregory has written a full-length memoir. *Papa: A Personal Memoir,* by Gregory H. Hemingway, M.D., (Boston: Houghton Mifflin Company, 1976) is a short book but, as Norman Mailer points out in his introduction, contains a powerful, clear-eyed portrait of a great and greatly troubled man who happened to be Gregory Hemingway's father. This is a story of fathers and sons and there is pain on nearly every page, but there is also love and great joy.

Mary Hemingway waited until 1976 to publish her autobiography. *How It Was,* by Mary Welsh Hemingway (New York: Alfred A. Knopf, 1976), is a long book that begins with a long, interesting section about Mary Welsh's life before she met Ernest Hemingway. A journalist herself, Mary Hemingway writes with honesty and pride of her marriage to a very difficult man, and reveals without false modesty the courageous good care she gave him as his body and his talent collapsed into sickness and paranoia.

BIOGRAPHICAL WORKS

Carlos Baker, Ph.D., is a Hemingway scholar, a fine critic, and a very good writer of prose. His biography, *Ernest Hemingway: A Life Story* (New York: Charles Scribner's Sons, 1969) remains, and seems likely to remain for quite a while, the definitive biography of Hemingway. The book is scrupulously objective and chronological, with an almost overwhelming body of documentation. Every biographer of Ernest Hemingway, whether scholarly or popular, must first offer thanks for Dr. Baker's abilities and discipline. *Ernest Hemingway: A Life Story* was deservedly a best-seller when it appeared, and its value has not diminished.

Another biographical best-seller was *Papa Hemingway: A Personal Memoir,* by A. E. Hotchner (New York: Random House, 1966). Hotchner, a journalist and television writer, grew close to Hemingway after World War II and accompanied him on many of his trips to Europe. *Papa Hemingway* created a sensation when it first appeared for its picture of Hemingway's decline. The book's accuracy has frequently been questioned, however, and it has a curious gossipy undertone. Readers might be warned to take Hotchner's memoir with a grain of salt.

Among less celebrated biographies, several are especially worthwhile:

Portrait of Hemingway, by Lillian Ross (New York: Simon & Schuster, 1961) was originally published in *The New Yorker* in 1951. A "new journalist" before that phrase was coined, Lillian Ross is a clear, funny writer whose portrait has enjoyed its share of controversy but which, according to many who knew

Hemingway, is a wonderfully accurate portrait of Ernest Hemingway at mid-century.

Papa: Hemingway in Key West 1928–1940, by James McLendon (Miami: E. A. Seamann Publishing, Inc., 1972), offers a close look at a dozen years in Hemingway's life and an equally close look at those same years in the life of Hemingway's home, Key West. Both portraits are well drawn, insightful, and accurate.

Hadley: The First Mrs. Hemingway, by Alice Hunt Sokoloff (New York: Dodd, Mead & Company, 1973), is of interest primarily for the long passages of quotation from Hadley Hemingway Mowrer.

Ernest Hemingway's life was documented photographically as well as literarily and there are three good collections of photographs, each with accompanying text:

Hemingway High on the Wild, by Lloyd Arnold (New York: Grosset & Dunlap Publishers, 1977), is a new edition of a book first published in 1968. The book was written, and most of its photographs taken, by Lloyd Arnold, photographer at Sun Valley during Hemingway's years there. The pictures show Hemingway the sportsman and celebrity, catching fish, shooting birds, and mingling with movie stars.

Ernest, by Peter Buckley (New York: The Dial Press, 1978), is divided into two sections around a long, subjective central essay. The photographs are all interesting and many of them are stunning. *Ernest* also contains photographs of corpses from Hemingway's photo collection.

Ernest Hemingway and His World, by Anthony Burgess (New York: Charles Scribner's Sons, 1978), is a slim book, holding not only photographs of Hemingway but also pictures of his peers, enemies, wives, children, homes, battlefields, and various editions of his work. Anthony Burgess is himself an important novelist who has been mentioned as a candidate for the Nobel Prize, and his thoughts on Ernest Hemingway's life, art, career, and influence are sound and thought-provoking.

CRITICAL WORKS

It is safe to say that more critical works have been written about Ernest Hemingway than about all but a few writers, and almost equally safe to assert that more critical nonsense has been written about Hemingway than about *any* writer. Readers approaching the body of Hemingway criticism should be careful, alert always to trust Hemingway's works more than works about those works.

Here, however, I would like to recommend two books that stand far above the rest of Hemingway criticism. One deals with Hemingway's fiction, the other with his nonfiction.

Carlos Baker is Hemingway's best biographer, and he is also one of his foremost critics. His *Hemingway: The Writer as Artist* (Princeton, N.J.: Princeton University Press, Fourth edition, 1972) was one of the earliest books about Hemingway's work and remains one of the most important and sensible.

Dr. Robert O. Stephens approached Hemingway's nonfiction for his definitive book, *Hemingway's Non-fiction: The Public Voice* (Chapel Hill, N.C.: University of North Carolina Press, 1968). Hemingway's nonfiction has been little treated, and that may well be because Dr. Stephens's work is so thoroughly sensible, exhaustive, and well written.

As for the rest of the world of Hemingway criticism, some is excellent, some good, much ludicrous. Read Hemingway instead.

THE WORKS OF
ERNEST HEMINGWAY

1923: *Three Stories and Ten Poems,* published privately by a small press in Paris.

1924: *in our time,* another small book privately published in Paris.

1925: *In Our Time,* Hemingway's first publication by a major American house.

1926: *The Torrents of Spring,* Hemingway's burlesque of Sherwood Anderson; the book Hemingway used to break his contract with Boni and Liveright and sign on with Scribners.

The Sun Also Rises (British title: *Fiesta*), Hemingway's first novel and first great popular success.

1927: *Men Without Women,* a collection of short stories.

1929: *A Farewell to Arms,* Hemingway's second novel; the book that consolidated his reputation as one of America's best young writers.

1932: *Death in the Afternoon,* Hemingway's book-length study of the bullfight.

1933: *Winner Take Nothing,* another collection of short stories.

1935: *Green Hills of Africa,* Hemingway's "nonfiction novel" telling the story of his first safari.

1937: *To Have and Have Not,* Hemingway's third novel; the only one of his novels to be set on American soil.

1938: *The Fifth Column and the First Forty-Nine Stories,*

Hemingway's only play along with the first collected edition of his short stories.

1940: *For Whom the Bell Tolls,* Hemingway's long novel of the Spanish Civil War; the book that made him rich.

1950: *Across the River and into the Trees,* Hemingway's fifth novel; generally considered his worst performance.

1952: *The Old Man and the Sea,* Hemingway's novella, which sold millions of copies in *Life* magazine and was equally successful as a book. This novella consolidated the opinion of the Nobel Prize committee.

1962: *The Wild Years,* a collection of Hemingway's very early journalism. Note: this book is not listed on the official publications list in the Scribners editions of Hemingway's works. *Published posthumously.*

1964: *A Moveable Feast,* Hemingway's sketches of life and struggle in Paris early in his career. *Published posthumously.*

1967: *By-Line: Ernest Hemingway,* journalism from throughout Hemingway's career. *Published posthumously.*

1969: *The Fifth Column and Four Stories of the Spanish Civil War,* a new edition of Hemingway's play along with four previously uncollected short stories. *Published posthumously.*

1970: *Islands in the Stream,* Hemingway's novel of the sea. *Published posthumously.*

1972: *The Nick Adams Stories,* a collection in chronological order with a variety of unpublished Adams material. *Published posthumously.*

1981: *Ernest Hemingway: Selected Letters, 1917–1961,* a huge collection of correspondence assembled by Dr. Carlos Baker. *Published posthumously.*

INDEX